Campus TO CORPORATE

Managing the Transition

ASHUTOSH SHARMA

V&S PUBLISHERS

Published by:

V&S PUBLISHERS

F-2/16, Ansari Road, Daryaganj, New Delhi-110002
  23240026, 23240027 • *Fax:* 011-23240028
Email: info@vspublishers.com

Branch : Hyderabad
5-1-707/1, Brij Bhawan (Beside Central Bank of India Lane)
Bank Street, Koti, Hyderabad - 500 095
  040-24737290
E-mail: vspublishershyd@gmail.com

Follow us on:

All books available at **www.vspublishers.com**

© **Copyright: Author**
ISBN 978-93-815885-9-8
Edition: 2012

Printed at: Param Offseters, Okhla, New Delhi-110020

Read this book if your answer to these questions is NO

❏ *Do you know what you need to learn and focus on to get that dream job?*

❏ *Do you know who do companies recruit?*

❏ *Do you know how to provide the answers interviewers look for?*

❏ *Do you know what changes you will face when you enter the work place?*

❏ *Do you know how to manage anxiety, stress, time, and relationships?*

❏ *Do you know how to manage difficult Bosses and Colleagues?*

❏ *Do you know which organisation type would suit you?*

❏ *Do you know how to build a network that will help you grow in career?*

❏ *Do you know how to grow in the organisation?*

Publisher's Note

Making the transition from College/ University Campus to Corporate World is one of the biggest challenges students face in their career as they confront an inevitable transition from the happy assignments and mid-semesters scenario to team work and deadlines. Moving from an academic environment to a corporate setting has many changes and one needs to understand the organisational dynamics in order to get well in this new environment as corporate houses prefer to recruit employees who can be immediately employed and deployed.

Training college/ university students to make them more employable is one of the key challenges for most of the companies across the world. So it is evident that companies also feel the necessity to groom the fresh students to make them more professional and fitted to a corporate setup and that is why companies organise various workshops to groom their employees. However, in most of the cases it is seen that these workshops end in incomplete training and disappointment.

Students and youngsters find it difficult to adapt the requirements of corporate environment primarily because of the vast difference in the way professors and managers operate; while professors focus on increasing learning quotient and improving subject matter understanding, managers want implementation of the knowledge and therefore focus on getting the task done, meeting deadlines, etc. So, while one focuses on learning, the other focuses on significant leverage. This added pressure takes a heavy toll on students and makes it even more difficult for them to scale the success ladder at corporate level. Besides handling these pressures, it is becoming more and more important to have the correct know-how to proceed in career.

To bridge the gap that exists between Campus environment and Corporate setting and to help those students who are just entering the Corporate World or in the threshold of Campus and Corporate, **V&S Publishers** has launched its imprint – **Campus to Corporate**.

This book has been written to make the young trainees aware of the changes that they should expect on the eventful transition from campus to corporate and hence help them set realistic expectations from work life. We hope this book will help readers not only prepare for the recruitment process but also cope with the challenges they face in work life and helps fresh graduates become better employees and professionals.

Contents

Acknowledgements

It is difficult to succeed in an endeavour without help and support from significant others. This book would not have been possible without the interest in books that my Father, **Sh. Onkar Dutt Sharma**, gave me in legacy and the numerous selfless sacrifices by my Mother, **Smt. Nirmala Sharma**.

I thank my wife **Ritu** for the constant inspiration and motivation through the ups and downs in my career and my little daughter **Ananya** and nephew **Aditya** for their smiles and affection which keep me energised and full of life.

My book would be incomplete without referring the names of my siblings – **Priyanka** and **Tarun**, in whose loving company I grew up.

I have been fortunate to have worked with **Mr. L Ravichandran,** my first Manager. I thank him for guiding me so well through the first two years of my career. I also can't thank enough **Mr. Andleeb Jain**, my friend, philosopher and guide, who has influenced my life in more than one way. I am forever indebted to him for all his kindness.

Learning can't happen without a Guru and I am lucky to have got at least two. I thank **Dr. S Swaminathan** for numerous little and big things that I learnt from him and also for igniting my passion in the field of Human Resources. I thank **Mr. PM Kumar**, who has been a constant source of inspiration for me. Listening to him speak for a minute is worth a thousand such books.

In the end I thank all Colleges and Institutes including my Alma Mater **Delhi College of Engineering** for continuously producing some of the best Engineers and Managers in the world despite the challenges that a developing nation like India faces.

Preface

Recently, I read a news article in a national daily: *Management Trainees Quit a Leading Public Sector Unit.* This organisation wanted to rejuvenate itself by bringing in these young people from leading premier institutes as change-agents. However, when the trainees went there, they found to their surprise that the treatment given to them was not what they had expected. As an outcome of resulting frustration they decided to quit. One can't single out who was responsible for it. The students joining the organisation were as much at fault for having unrealistic expectations as the organisation was for not setting expectations right. This is an example of what usually happens with Management and Engineer trainees: Unmet expectations resulting in frustrations. Most of them, therefore, usually leave their first company within a year or two.

From being a Management trainee myself to handling Management and Engineer trainees, I have been for the last ten years exposed to the challenges faced by them both in securing a job that suits their personality, skills and aspirations, and then in adapting themselves to the change they encounter when they join their first job. So, when my publisher contacted me early this year for writing a book on this subject, it was a very easy and eager *"Yes"* from me. I thought it a really good opportunity for me to reach students and fresh Management and Engineer trainees and share certain facts and techniques with them to cope better with this transition; and, hence this book in your hands today. This book has been written to make the young trainees aware of the changes that they should expect and hence help them set realistic expectations from work life.

As I interacted with different institutes and colleges as part of my job, I realised that they are now much more sensitised to the challenges of campus-to-corporate transition than what they were a decade ago. Despite the commendable efforts of those institutes, I still find students lacking in their adaptive skills when they come to work. I found less was being done to address this adaptive challenge. Though, I am dealing with both pre-placement and post-placement scenarios in this book, it is the second part which differentiates this book from most others.

I hope this book helps fresh graduates become better employees and professionals and helps the Indian Economy keep growing at an ever-increasing pace.

"Your time is limited, so don't waste it living someone else's life. Don't be trapped by dogma – which is living with the results of other people's thinking. Don't let the noise of other's opinions drown out your own inner voice. And most important: Have the courage to follow your heart and intuition. They somehow already know what you truly want to become. Everything else is secondary."

— **Steve Jobs**

Introduction

The Job of Getting a Job

The profession a person practices has a big say in definition of his overall personality. I have often noticed (and, I am sure you would also have) that while meeting new people, one among a first few questions is – *What do you do*? Or, *where do you work*? In fact we fall victim to this obsessive question immediately after coming to this mortal planet. Parents usually insist the priests and astrologers to predict what would the child do when he grows up. This curiosity doesn't die down so easily. Parents keep asking the child again and again – *"What do you want to do when you grow up*?" Each comment from the teacher is taken with an intention to predict which particular area a child excels in. Each exam a child writes becomes an assessment for how good the child would be in getting a job. And, each activity of the child is observed for some hidden talent.

In India students often take a decision to pursue a particular career by the time they write their class 10th exam. There is a pretty big industry out there helping students prepare for various competitive examinations. Few of these aspirants get into coveted institutes and are assured of being placed in plush paying jobs and others get into not-so-premier institutes and prepare hard to enter the competitive job market. Whatever the route be, we invest close to 30% of our lives just preparing to be into a profession and thus it is no surprise that it plays such a big part in defining our personality. Moreover, what we do in a few years before getting a job and for a next few years after getting the job is massively instrumental in deciding how we spend the rest of our lives.

India's higher education system is third largest in the world with more than 316 Central and State Universities, 129 Deemed Universities and 90 Private Universities[1]. There are more than 16000 colleges and institutes in which are enrolled more than 80 thousand students. Interestingly, most of the corporates are unanimously of the view that a very scant percentage of this population is really employable. In an international study conducted by McKinsey in 2008, it was reported that only 25% of Engineers, 15% of Finance/ Accounting professionals, and 10% of other general candidates are suitable for jobs that Indian Companies have to offer[2]. The 11th five year plan noted that in institutes providing vocational and technical education the quality of training provided was a concern[3]. The primary purpose of our institutes, universities, colleges is to impart academic knowledge and most of them are not able to even do that properly before they could prepare the students for handling the real life problems at the workplace.

Missing the point

Primed by the way our educational institutes approach education, the preparation that we put in to get that dream job and to be successful in it is focused singularly on academics. Academics only define one part of any job – 'What'. The other important part – 'How to' – is often left to experience – a tough and slow teacher. In fact the content or the "what" part, coupled with general preparation for Group Discussions (GD) and Interviews, helps us to get the job; and, perhaps, that is why getting a job is often an easier part. The difficult part is to sustain and progress in the job once you get it. Any performance at the work-place is delivered on the contextual background of human systems. The "How to" part thus refers to the way a person navigates through this system to deliver the performance. It includes working in a team, understanding needs of others, communicating effectively with others, understanding culture, making decisions in ambiguous situations, managing emotions, managing relationships, etc. These skills are learnt by the part of the brain entrenched deep down. It learns only in the presence of commitment, concerted practice, and constant feedback[4]. Once on the job people often take time to come up to the learning curve and start performing.

Further, if the focus is too much on getting a job, the long term goal of career development might be jeopardised. There is a definite difference between getting a job and making a career. Job is a snap-shot but career is a live motion film. I define career to have five irreducible components:

Feeling of being
successful

Identity

Passion

Decent
livelihood **CAREER** Contribution to
the society

1. It should help you discover and develop an identity
2. It should ignite passion in you
3. It should contribute value to the society
4. It should provide you a decent living
5. It should make you feel successful

In my opinion a career that lacks any of these is employment and not career in the real sense.

Human beings differ from other organisms, so far science believes, in being able to remember the past and visualise the future. Most other organisms stay perpetually locked in the present. This capability is no small gift to mankind. It is because of this capability that we can imagine the results of our decisions in distant future. However, despite this wonderful gift many of us don't utilise it while taking the job related decisions and end up in leading suboptimal lives.

Two phases in the journey

Before starting this book I went through a few books that have been written earlier on the subject and I found that a lot of emphasis there is put on the first half of the journey – *getting the job* and the second part – *on the job* – is given a secondary treatment. I don't undermine the effort that those books put for providing useful tips for preparing getting into the world of work. The tips and techniques offered are quite useful and can really help an aspirant get a good job. However, I feel that this is the same cardinal mistake

Table 1.1

	Job-Seeker Student	Fresher Employee
Academic Vs Practical Learning	Academic scores, scholastic achievements	Adaptability, Learning from Experience, Impression Management
Performance Criteria	Performance in Technical/Aptitude Tests, GD, Interviews	Performance in ambiguous situations, motivating self, stress management
Social Skills	Extracurricular activities	Team work, interpersonal relationships
Emotional Range	Aspiration Geneses: Self-doubt, anxiety about future, stress due to pressure from family and peer-pressure and so on.	Reality Perception Geneses: Confusion, apprehension, alienation, depression, stress, anxiety of learning, and so on.

that our academic institutes are guilty of: *Not preparing the students for the "How to" part of the job.*

The geneses of emotions that a job-seeker goes through and that a newcomer faces are very different. While one prepares for getting a job, the emotions have genesis in aspirations but while in the job the genesis of emotions is in situations one is face-to-face with. The emotions – anxiety, apprehension, depression, stress – while preparing for the job are because of self-assessment of adequacy of academic and interview process skills. In the job, however, same emotions – anxiety, apprehension, depression, stress – are because of adaptability issues. The adaptability skills thus require a special treatment in a book that claims to be the succor of a fresher.

Keeping this view in mind I have divided the book in two parts, which have a logical sequence but emotional disconnect. The former deals with aspirations and emotions associated with it, while the latter deals with emotions that one encounters when one is face-to-face with the reality quite different from expectations.

Book's Intention

Mullah Nasiruddin was returning home from his work one night. He saw a man bent over his knees and searching frantically for something below the street lamp. A good Samaritan that he was, Mullah Nasiruddin went to the hapless looking guy and asked him, "What are your searching for, Brother?" "My keys," he replied. "Oh! I see. Let me also help you then." Mullah also joined him in his search. After searching desperately for 10 minutes Mullah gave up. He asked him again, "Where the hell did you drop it?"There below that tree," he pointed to a tree 100 meters from the street lamp. "Why the heck are you searching here then?" "Because light is here only; it's dark over there," he replied innocently.

Though the idiocy of the desperate key searcher is very obvious in this example, humans have a dismal record of focusing only on available information (below the lamp) and totally disregarding the information that is not in front of eyes (in darkness, below the tree). Absence doesn't draw our attention[5]. It is called *Omission Bias*. Learning thus takes place in four steps:

Unconscious Incompetence: *I don't know that I am bad at adapting to change* (because I have never faced change)

Conscious Incompetence: *I know that I am bad at adapting to change* (because I have to live in hostel without the comforts of home)

Conscious competence: *I practice the new skills consciously* (I try consciously to become more accommodating with other students)

Unconscious competence: *Because of continuous practice I demonstrate these skills without conscious effort* (When I get a job, I am naturally accommodating to other colleagues)

Students often do not know what they lack (absence of knowledge) so they are not able to take effective decisions in choosing a career or prepare effectively for either the campus placements or the challenges of first job. They follow whatever is visible to them – peers, relatives, recruitment trends, popular choices, etc. This type of preparation might or might not lead a person to a desirable goal. Keeping this challenge in view this book has a three-fold purpose:

1. *Making the reader aware of the areas that are important and need focus in the journey.*
2. *Bringing in a level of self-awareness about the reader's degree of readiness vis-à-vis those areas and developing a felt need for development.*
3. *Providing tools and techniques for working towards improvement.*

To avoid the approach and discussion becoming too general the first part of the book is primarily written for students who are currently doing professional courses like Engineering, Management, Law, etc. The basic assumption thus is that the reader has made a choice of profession already. So, the book will not discuss about how to select the profession that might fit you. The discussion, on which type of career to choose within a particular profession would, however, be there. Also, I am aware of the fact that many students realise that they would have done better in some other field only after they have spent some time in a professional college. For such students the realisation comes because of the self-discovery that they go through during the course of the academic program. I assume that the self-discovery and a will to succeed in such people is sufficient to take them further on their desired path and they can consider reading only those portions of the book that are generally applicable to all individuals.

The book is written in a conversationalist style. It begins with a small dip-stick assessment to see your preparation level. All topics that talk about preparation are accompanied with tools that can be easily used by the readers to guide their preparation. Several situations are quoted to highlight the challenges that a new comer faces at work.

Growth and Development, however, is a choice. The final decision to go ahead with the preparation lies solely with the reader.

The book is divided into two parts:

1. On Campus

The movement from school to college provides the students with a lot of independence and liberty. No longer do they have to wear the same uniform everyday or say morning prayers in the assembly or attend classes back-to-back like you did in school. There is an opportunity to impress friends with latest fashion accessories, mobile phones, cars and bikes; opportunity to bunk classes and go out to movies, restaurants, and shopping malls with friends; opportunity to experiment with new lifestyles and so on.

This is also an opportunity for them to choose which subjects they want to pursue for study further; which career they want to embark upon; and which organisation they want to see yourself in. This time usually is the differentiating factor between successful and not-so-successful job seekers. Starting preparation early provides a distinct competitive advantage. As the time for placement approaches it is time to do a few last minute preparations only.

Some challenges before a student vis-à-vis getting a job are:

- *Which career to choose? Which companies to opt for?*
- *How to prepare for assessment tests, group discussions, and interviews?*
- *How to manage stress?*

The book begins with a reality check to assess the readiness level of the reader to undertake this journey. As mentioned earlier it is one beam of light in the dark area below the tree (under which the keys were lost).

Once the reader has understood what his readiness level is for entering the job market in general, it is very important that he understands his penchants, gifts, and strengths early on. **Chapter 3** will help the reader take steps toward increasing self-awareness. The resulting awareness can help him pursue a career that will be enriching and satisfying. Moreover, understanding oneself in terms of personality, interests, and values helps in a variety of other ways as well –

- Self-aware people choose areas that complement their interests and personalities
- Self-aware people do not compromise with their values and thus avoid the pain of dissonance.
- Self-aware people have clear goals. Clear goals are more achievable and motivate us more than vague undefined goals.

   – Self-aware people can, once in job, sculpt their jobs to suit their personalities, skills, and interests and thus are more satisfied than others.

Getting to know where one stands and identifying where one wants to go is useless if there is no structured development plan. In fact writing the goals down actually increases one's chances of achieving them. Chapters 3 will also introduce the reader to a design format of a development plan.

Companies that visit professional institutions usually have a select set of criteria that students need to fulfill for getting selected. The format is usually similar for most companies.

1. Academic qualifications and scores
2. Technical Test
3. Aptitude Test
4. Group Discussion
5. Personal Interviews
6. Psychometric Test

Knowing what companies look for before they put candidates through this rigmarole is the key to making it through the final round. **The chapters 4, 5 and 6** deal with this process and take the reader inside the mind of the recruiter. This chapter also focuses on how recruiters also commit very human errors which one needs to be very careful about. This selection process is not 100% efficient and one might be unlucky enough to be screened out in the first round itself. These chapters advise on how to minimise that odd.

2. On the Job

The first day at job is preserved very carefully in our memories. All of us have several stories to share of our experiences in the first few formative years at our first company. The freedom that we enjoyed during college time proves but ephemeral. Now there is again (at least for most of us) a fixed time to come and go, designated lunch hours, tea-breaks, discipline (and, for some even uniforms again). But this loss of freedom is not the end of the story; the worst is yet to come. There are *deliverables with clear time-lines, extended hours at work, politics, uncooperative colleagues, nagging boss, ...*the list is endless.

The transition from campus-to-corporate is one streaked with many ambiguities too. You find that deliverables with clear timelines at college were much more palatable than the undefined deliverables with timelines that ended yesterday. You realise that bosses who give you a lot of work are much better than ones who would micromanage and hardly give you space to breath. There are languages full of abbreviations, jargons, and your ears pain hearing them. There are no clear answers to the obscure practical questions that will stare at you till you start feeling that your entire academic endeavour was a sheer waste of time. Chapter 7 lets the reader broadly see what changes does the transition to the work bring along.

The time now is one where one needs to adopt an entirely new way of learning. Learning now takes place through *"Experiential"* route – where each experience becomes a seed for new learning. One is now face-to-face with new expectations that were never asked for before this time – *Time management, Self-Guided-Learning, Self-Discipline, Self-Motivation, Humility, Adherence to process, Alignment to goals,* etc. **Chapter 8** will discuss and explicate these changes and then share the techniques to effectively deal with them

The big change will also be accompanied by a cocktail of emotions. **Chapter 9** will discuss the reasons for anxiety, apprehensions, and stress at the work place in the first few months. We will look at different ways of dealing with these sources of stress and anxiety. We will then build on how cognitive techniques like knowing one's emotional triggers, reappraising situations, labeling emotions can lead to better emotional management in this phase.

Managing one's time and goals is one of the biggest challenges in any job. **Chapter 10** will discuss techniques to best manage time and deliver results.

Chapters 11 will acquaint the reader with some universal organisational cultural and structural typologies. There has been a lot of work that Organisation Psychologists have done in identifying these typologies. The organisation that the students eventually join might be of any of these types. The knowledge in these chapters will help the reader to do due diligence before making the decision to finally join a company.

Man is a social animal. He needs others to get his work done. One needs new relationships upon entering the worklife. These relationships have to be consciously built and nurtured. **Chapter 12** will help the reader in building a network of working relationships that will further help in getting work done through others.

In all this topsy-turvydomone also has to focus on career growth. Deciding which area to focus more on? What to learn? What to excel in? What to avoid? Who to approach? Who to make mentor? And so on. These questions are central to career planning and one needs to focus attention on them while being bombarded from all the sideswith demands, timelines and deliverables. The last **chapter 13** thus will focus on how the reader may guide himself in his career journey

PART 1
ON CAMPUS

Getting Ready

This book is based on the belief that practice can trump talent. Nothing can beat an early, steady, and dedicated preparation. Hubris is at the root of failures of many talented people who otherwise had immense potential.

In this section of the book we will discuss about gaining an early lead in developing oneself for a successful career.

CHAPTER 1

Dipstick

My first job after my Graduation was that of a Maintenance Engineer in a process plant. The organisation at that time was preparing for applying for a prestigious award for Quality Management. Quality improvement, I learnt there, can't start until we measure where we stand today – You can't improve if you don't measure. This statement was very simple and being an engineer and having studied Instrumentation and Control as a subject, I was aware of the importance of measurement. But, I had never realised that it could be put in this way. I remember huge improvements – step-by-step – that the plant was able to achieve just because they were measuring their effectiveness on the way.

The importance of measurement was making sense to me for improving quality in process plants. But I was still looking at the entire thing as an engineer. It was when I read – *"The Fifth Discipline"* by *Peter Senge*, that I made one more leap. I realised two things:

1. *Measurement is necessary for self-improvement also.*
2. *Measurement not only gives you a picture of your current reality but along with your vision provides you with enough motive force to move forward.*

So, here also we start with measuring how much are we prepared for taking on the journey from campus to corporate.

In this chapter you will go through a series of self-assessments designed to give a peek into yourself. I have the following assessments for you:

- How well do I know the campus selection process?
- How well do I know the world of corporate?
- Am I preparing enough?

Assessment 1
How well do I know the campus selection process?

Put True or False against each statement (answers provided in Annexure 1)

1. No amount of practice can prepare you enough for assessment tests and group discussions. Either you have it or you don't.

2. Companies recruit from campuses because it is cost-effective to build an internal cadre of employees that could grow up to leadership levels than to hire from outside.

3. Technical and aptitude tests are tools for rejection rather than selection.

4. Group Discussion is often a tool for rejection rather than selection.

5. The first person to start the group-discussion always gets selected.

6. You should speak the most to get selected in the Group Discussion.

7. You should always try to moderate the discussion.

8. You should always agree with what others are saying in a Group Discussion.

9. No amount of preparation can help you make through an interview. You are either made for a job or not.

10. You should not eat anything before technical or aptitude test.

11. Interview panelists are always rational in their selection criteria.

12. Panelists have a structured format for interview.

13. Telling panelists about your personal problems (poverty, disabilities, etc.) may decrease the chance of getting selected.

14. Panelists are impressed by fluent English and communication skills.

15. Panelists should talk more than you, so they would not like you if you speak more.

16. It might matter if you give your resume in a heavy folder to the interviewer.

17. If you fake pose of a confident person it might actually increase your confidence.

18. You should write all those desirable traits in your resume that are found commonly in other resumes.

19. Interview panelists don't read the resume for framing questions.

20. It is required to convince others of your ideas in a Group Discussion.

Assessment 2
How well do I know the world of corporate?

Put True of False against each statement (answers provided in Annexure 1)

1. In smaller organisations roles and responsibilities are clearly defined because of less number of employees.

2. Responsibilities are given to those employees who ask for it. So you should ask for as much responsibilities as possible in the first year itself.

3. All organisations provide clear goals to the employees.

4. Organisations are rational and technical structures, decisions here are not based on emotions.

5. All managers provide work to newcomers based on their qualification.

6. All organisations follow the espoused values and beliefs.

7. Business organisations exist to make profits; they have no social responsibility.

8. Career development of employees is the responsibility of the organisation.

9. Anybody can adapt to any type of organisation culture.

10. Organisations expect immediate contribution from the newcomers from the campus.

11. The performance rating after appraisal is based on achievement of your goals only.

12. Anxiety and stress always dilute your performance.

13. In case a colleague spreads rumours about you, it is advisable that you take action at a personal level.

14. It is possible to perform most of the jobs independently without help from others. So don't focus much on building relationships at job.

15. More the number of connections you have, better it is in organisations.

16. A quick vertical growth is better than the one that consists of a mix of lateral moves also.

17. If you help everybody, you get only help in return.

18. You should never ask for feedback from your boss before performance appraisal.

19. You should never say *No* to any work assigned to you.

20. You should decide your priority list based on urgency.

Assessment 3
Am I preparing enough?

Give 1 mark to yourself for each 'YES" (Be Honest)

1. I have done an objective assessment of my strengths through psychometric tests or extensive feedback from others.

2. I know what my top-3 strengths are and I can give you examples to support my belief.

3. I have shortlisted the companies that I would like to join.

4. I know which function will best suit me.

5. I have interacted with my senior batch-mates to understand the type of questions that the companies in my shortlist ask in interviews.

6. I read newspapers everyday from cover-to-cover.

7. I read at least 1 book per month apart from my course books.

8. I participate in mock Group Discussions and Mock Interviews.

9. The mock GDs and Interviews that I participated in were observed by a neutral observer who gave me objective feedback for improvement.

10. I ask for feedback from my peers/elders/seniors.

11. I have written down a plan for developing the competencies that I lack.

12. I have participated in training programs/workshops for developing competencies as per my plan.

13. I am confident that I will have all the skills required to be successful in the corporate world.

14. I am confident that I will get the job that I want.

15. I will accept only that job-offer which gives me the type of profile that I want.

16. I have realistic expectations from my work life developed based on my discussions with people who are currently working.

17. I know what different organisation structures are and which one suits me best.

18. I know how to adapt myself to the changes that I would encounter in transition from college to work.

19. I master techniques for managing stress and emotions.

20. I know how to expedite experiential learning.

CHAPTER 2

Who are you?
How knowing oneself improves one's chances of getting a job

Successful careers are not planned. They develop when people are prepared for opportunities because they know their strengths, their method of work, and their values.

— **Peter Drucker**

Had AR Rahman tried to make a career in cricket and Sachin Tendulkar in music, you can't be sure if you would have known those great names today. They could achieve stellar successes in their careers because they chose the turf where they could deliver their best.

I made a comment in the Introduction chapter – *this book is being written for people who are doing professional courses and hence they have already made a career choice to some extent.* However, I should highlight the fact that I, personally, know people who finished their degrees in Engineering and then went on to study law to enter a legal career or to enter publishing industry to become editors and publishers. People often realise the unique gifts that they have after they chose to enter a certain profession. It is never too late, however. It is better late than never.

The Journey Inside

The first step towards making a successful career is 'Understanding Self'. Works by famous psychologists like *Holland[1]*, *CG Jung[2]*, *Alfred Adler* have shown that people fall in different personality types predisposing them to different types of career choices. Complementary personality types and job requirements result in better results at job[3]. Further work by *Howard Gardner[4]* has shown that people also have different types of *smartness* (Intelligence). These types also decide in which particular area a person is likely to excel. Besides personality types and intelligence, which are largely determined by birth or by early childhood experiences, there are other factors also that make each one of us distinct and unique.

The job of finding the job therefore should begin with self-discovery. For the purpose of easy analysis I have divided the question "*Who am I?*" in four sub-questions that might influence selection of our career and our performance in it. The four questions are given in the figure No. 2.1

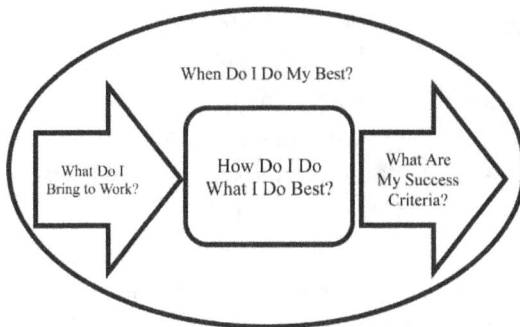

Four Components of the Question
"WHO AM I?"

Figure 2.1

What do I bring to work?

Each career puts in specific demands on the person pursuing it. These demands may be: **Personality traits** – the innate propensities, tendencies that are relatively stable over a period of time, for example: introversion-extraversion, dominance-submissiveness, controlling-influencing, cautious-liberal, etc.; **Special abilities** – abilities to solve problems and create socially valuable products, for example: Logical, Linguistic, Musical abilities, etc.; **Skills** – knowledge or learnt abilities through experience or apprenticeships, for example: computer, engineering, medical, Skills, etc.; and finally, **Values and Beliefs** - the internal guidelines and beliefs about what is right or wrong and how things work, for example: Truth, Trust, Work-life balance, ethics, etc.

Before you make a career decision you need to discover which of the personality traits, special abilities, skills or values and beliefs you bring to job.

Let's deal with them one-by-one.

Personality Types

"An Introvert Salesman", "A Shy Actor", "A Restless Clerk", "An Arrogant Waiter", "A Cautious Writer" – all these have one thing in common: they are all oxymoron. The personality adjectives here are not the usual stereotypes that you will have of those professions. It is anybody's guess that these odd combinations of profession and personality traits will be utter failures. Personality Traits are consistent, stable and innate behavioural characteristics that people demonstrate in their relationship with the world. There is a general agreement among psychologists and career counselors that people who choose career according to their specific personality traits are usually happier, satisfied and more fulfilled in their jobs[3].

But contrary to what you thought about the oxymoron given above, you should note that personality, as measured using psychometric tests, and success at work place are not tightly related. It means that you might be successful at the workplace even though you don't have the exact personality to suit that particular job. Despite the natural propensities, instincts, desires, etc., people have a remarkable capacity to demonstrate desirable behaviours when it matters. A husband who shouts at his wife at home would think multiple times before doing so with his boss. An arrogant neighbour might be a very courteous hotel manager. It is because success at work place depends more on demonstrated behaviours and competencies that consist of attributes like knowledge and technical skills besides personality traits. Behaviours are learnable and trainable. But make no mistake; the personality type is a determinant of how much you enjoy your work, what level of excellence you achieve in it and what legacy you leave behind.

In a recent survey[5] conducted by Dr. Marshall Goldsmith, he asked people to divide their work in three categories – Play, the part of your work which you enjoy doing and would do even without pay; Work, the part of your work you don't enjoy doing but would do for a pay; Misery, the part of your work which you don't like to do even for a pay. Dr. Goldsmith reports that business executives feel that 15% of their work is Play, 75% is Work, and 10% is Misery. I guess it depicts what percentage of their work is aligned, what is slightly aligned, and what is completely out of alignment, with their personality traits in that order.

There are different typologies of personality, each with its own theory and psychometric instrument. I would take you through just one of the more popular ones here. However, before we start discussing any further, I would strongly suggest that you take up a validated tool for arriving at your personality type. I would not resort to providing any indicative personality test here because developing these tests is a long and scientific process. It takes years to create a validated, reliable test and then too – not a single test can predict a personality with 100% accuracy.

Holland Personality Types

Dr. John Holland is Professor Emeritus at *John Hopkins University*. He has done a lot of research in identifying job-relevant personality traits and satisfaction. His research indicated that people naturally fall in six (6) personality categories that define which jobs are suitable for them.

Holland also stated:

○ *People with similar personality types get attracted to each other.*

○ *There are six types of work environments also.*

○ *People who choose careers in their types of environment are more successful and happy.*

The six categories are:

i. **Realistic** – This type of people like work that requires physical, technical, or athletic skills. They like working with their hands, tools or machines, etc.

ii. **Investigative** – This is scientific type. These people like to know, analyse, investigate, and observe. They like work where abstract thinking and creative problem solving is required.

iii. **Artistic** – They like unrestricted creativity, using imagination. They like work where originality in writing, language, design or product is required.

iv. **Social** – This type is humanistic, team oriented and concerned with welfare of others. They like working with people in educating, training, enlightening or helping them.

v. **Enterprising** – This type likes influencing and leading others. They like work where they could sell, persuade or motivate others.

vi. **Conventional** – This type enjoys highly repetitive, official, administrative or clerical job. They like work which offers high structure, data crunching, dealing with numbers and conformance to an established plan.

Though these personality types were devised keeping the US culture in mind, it has been applied generally in other countries as well. These categories are pure types and people usually are a mixture of a few dominant and supporting types. The types are represented in a hexagon. In the hexagon, the adjacent types share some characteristics and the opposing types have opposing characteristics. Different combinations of personality styles (called Holland Codes) lend themselves to different families of jobs and careers. Dr. Holland asserts that the satisfaction, happiness and the success that a person derives out of his job depends a great deal on the fit between the personality type and the job family. The hexagon representing the personality types and their characteristics is given in the *figure no. 2.2*

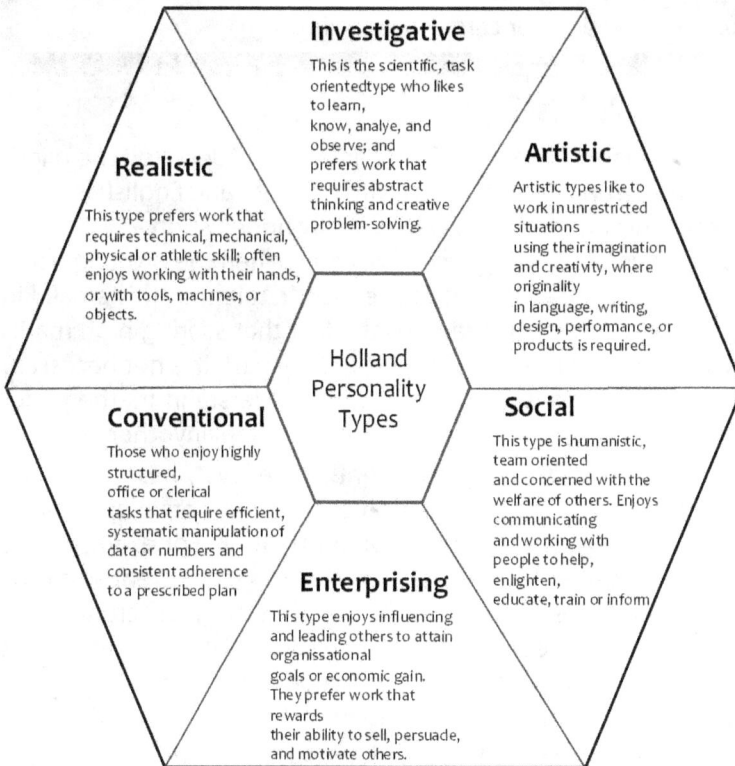

Investigative
This is the scientific, task orientedtype who likes to learn, know, analye, and observe; and prefers work that requires abstract thinking and creative problem-solving.

Realistic
This type prefers work that requires technical, mechanical, physical or athletic skill; often enjoys working with their hands, or with tools, machines, or objects.

Artistic
Artistic types like to work in unrestricted situations using their imagination and creativity, where originality in language, writing, design, performance, or products is required.

Holland Personality Types

Conventional
Those who enjoy highly structured, office or clerical tasks that require efficient, systematic manipulation of data or numbers and consistent adherence to a prescribed plan

Social
This type is humanistic, team oriented and concerned with the welfare of others. Enjoys communicating and working with people to help, enlighten, educate, train or inform

Enterprising
This type enjoys influencing and leading others to attain organissational goals or economic gain. They prefer work that rewards their ability to sell, persuade, and motivate others.

Figure 2.2

Exhibit 2.1

Other Popular Psychometric Questionnaires

1. MBTI: This is most widely used psychometric questionnaire. Millions of people take this test every year. The test is based on a rather esoteric theory developed by one of the most influential psychologists of all times – Dr. CG Jung.

2. DISC: This is another popular instrument. It differs from others as it focuses more on demonstrated behaviours rather innate and diffi cult to observe personality traits.

3. 16PF: This test has 16 Global Personality Factors. It is again an elaborate instrument and is used widely for career counseling.

What Gifts Do I have?

The popular Hindi movie "Tare Zameen Par" depicted the plight of little Ishaan, who struggled with his Math and English lessons. His parents and teachers were equally hopeless on any chances of improvement in this kid. It was only when the protagonist in the movie notices the immense artistic talent in this small kid that the audience also realises the fact that scoring high marks in academics is not the only way to be smart. It is not necessary that if you are not smart enough to understand mathematics and verbal skills you will also not be smart in anyother way.

In fact our brain, many scientists believe[6], has a modular structure. There are different parts of human brain specialised for processing different types of information. For example, the area responsible for linguistic capabilities is different from the area responsible for artistic gifts. We, thus, have different brains within the brain, each brain handling different intelligence in its own right. The talent that a person possesses depends on the area which is more developed in his brain.

Howard Gardner is an influential cognitive psychologist who came with the revolutionary idea of Multiple Intelligence. In a line of analysis that he carried out chiefly between 1970-

1980, he developed the theory of Multiple Intelligence. This perspective is basically a critique of the singular, rigid view of intelligence that was in general circulation among public during that time (and even now).

The general view of intelligence as most of us understand is that:

1. Intelligence is a single entity
2. People are born with a certain amount of intelligence
3. The amount of intelligence we have is determined by our genes and can't be changed
4. IQ tests predict the amount of intelligence one has

Howard Gardner followed an eclectic, interdisciplinary approach while studying Anthropology, Evolution, and Neuroscience to reach the conclusion that intelligence couldnot be defined with such a tunnel view as had been adopted by those championing IQ tests as the ultimate measure of human intelligence. He says that Intelligence is a capability to process specific type of information in certain ways to solve problems or fashion products. To be considered intelligent these products must be considered valuable in at least one culture or community.

There have been critics of Multiple Intelligence (MI) theory, as have been for many ideas that go beyond the ordinary way of thinking, but Multiple Intelligence has stood those to emerge as one of the most influential theories of human intelligence[7]. The application of MI in schools and other educational institutes has been very successful.

In short, Gardener proposes that there are at least 8 types of smartness or intelligence that exist in humans. These intelligences also interact with each other and with the society to process information and create products that are valued within a culture or outside a particular culture.

These intelligences are:

I. **Logical/Mathematical**: Ability to understand and process numbers and logic. This intelligence is usually prominent in people like Scientists, Mathematicians, Analysts, Detectives, Accountants, Engineers, Teachers, Professors, etc.

II. **Linguistic**: This refers to the ability to deal effectively with language – both spoken and written. This intelligence manifests itself in people like Writers, Editors, Poets, Corporate Trainers, Radio-jockeys, MCs, etc.

III. **Musical:** This refers to the ability to understand and create musical pieces. People possessing this intelligence can be very popular and successful in the field of music.

IV. **Bodily-Kinesthetic:** This is the ability to understand and manipulate one's body. Actors, Sports Persons, Dancers, etc., demonstrate this type of intelligence.

V. **Spatial**: This smartness endows one to be able to visualise and imagine shapes and manipulate them in their minds. Artists, Painters, Architects, Designers, Sculptors, and Civil Engineers, etc., are the people with this smartness.

VI. **Naturalist**: This smartness enables a person to understand and appreciate nature in unique ways. People with this intelligence are often successful in the areas of Geology, Forestry, Poultry, Farming, Ornithology, Zoology, etc.

VII. **Interpersonal**: This smartness contributes to the capability to build and manage fruitful relationships with other people. This is one type of intelligence which is required to be successful in most of the professions. But there are some professions where this is indispensible – Sales, Hospitality, Human Resources, Event Management, etc.

VIII. **Intrapersonal:** This smartness again is required for internal growth and is of paramount importance when it comes to achieving success in general life. It refers to how much a person is conscious of his own strengths, weaknesses, motives, values and beliefs. In fact the primary purpose of this chapter is around this smartness only.

Though there are several paper and pencil tests available for measuring your MI levels, for the purpose of this book I would assume that mere awareness about the existence of these intelligences should be enough for you to guess your own levels in these intelligences. In many of the workshops that I have conducted where I used a test in conjunction with people's own perception of their intelligence levels in MI model, I found their guesses to be quite accurate. You may, however, take one of several tests available online and transfer your score here in the table below.

Table 2.1

Intelligence	Score (0-10)	Intelligence	Score(0-10)
Logical/Mathematical		Spatial	
Linguistic		Naturalist	
Bodily Kinesthetic		Interpersonal	
Musical		Intrapersonal	

Exhibit 2.2

How understanding your Gifts can help you progress in your career

Rajeev finished his B.Com and had to join a job as a data-entry operator in a company. He couldn't pursue his higher education because of financial reasons. He did this job with sincerity and was praised by his supervisor for meticulous job. But, this job was not something that he enjoyed doing. The monotony of the job was demotivating. One day his supervisor asked him to help him design a poster for an event that their department was organising. He did a fantastic job and his supervisor praised him for his fine understanding of colour combinations and graphic design. While designing the poster, Rajeev realised that this is a job that he would enjoy doing because he had a natural knack for it. He also recalled several drawing competitions that he had won during school times.

Motivated by this experience he requested his supervisor to try for his transfer to the Graphic Design team in the Corporate Communications department. His supervisor understood Rajeev's penchant for design and helped him navigate to become a Graphic Designer.

What knowledge and skills do I have?

You also need to take stock of the knowledge and skills that you possess in order to see which type of job would suit you.

Skills could be divided into three types: Technical Skills, which you get through professional training and which helps you perform only a particular technical and functional job (Accounting, Engineering, IT, Human Resources, Designing, etc); Transferrable skills, which are required across most of the jobs (Communication skills, Analytical Ability, Budgeting, Ideating, Problem Solving, etc); and finally, Adaptive skills, which are required to succeed against some very human challenges in all types of jobs (Stress Management, Emotional Management, Conflict Management, Building Trust, Networking, Persuasiveness, Time Management, Working in teams, etc).

Similarly, Knowledge that you possess by virtue of your education and experience can also be divided into two types: Declarative Knowledge, which consists of facts and data based knowledge that you usually acquire from books or classroom study and answers to the question *what?*; and, Procedural Knowledge, which consists of procedures and processes of doing things and answers to the question *how?*

In the table below take stock of your knowledge and skills.

Table 2.2

SKILL/KNOWLEDGE	I have following skills/knowledge
Technical Skills	
Transferrable Skills	
Adaptive Skills	
Declarative Knowledge	
Procedural Knowledge	

What are my values and beliefs?

Ashok was a young engineer. It was his first job straight from college. He was responsible for maintenance of a production area in a process plant. One day while an electrician was working under his supervision at an electrical feeder, the electrician switched off a feeder supplying power to a running machine. This small mistake resulted in a lot of waste production. Ashok had two options; first to hide the reason for the tripping of the machine to some problem inside it or to accept the mistake of the electrician working under his supervision. He chose the latter. The production head commended his courage to accept it in front of everyone while he could conveniently hide it from everybody, which was a norm in this plant as production and maintenance departments played a game for pushing responsibility for waste production to each other. However, Ashok's boss, when he came to know of this incident, told Ashok that honesty didn't mean standing naked. With such practices rampant in the plant, Ashok finally decided to leave the company and move on.

What happened with Ashok was a case of clashing values and beliefs. Values and Beliefs are our internal guidelines that help us take decisions when we are in dilemmatic situations. Our beliefs are our conviction on what is right and what is wrong. Values, on the other hand, tell us what is important to us and in what rank order. We have value ranking for our beliefs also. It means some of our beliefs are more important to us than others. For example, in the above case Ashok believed that one should do his best to be successful in one's career. He also believed that one should be honest in his pursuance of career goals. His second belief by definition took precedence over the first belief. And, that's why he decided to leave this job and move on exploring other career options.

In your pursuit of a right career path you should be clear on what are the values and beliefs that these career paths work with. Values are often related with beliefs about personal behaviours but beliefs also could be about interpersonal relationships, spirituality, ethics and morals, life-style, environmental issues, social causes, etc. A clarification at an earlier stage helps you avoid the pain of working at a place where you would have to compromise with your value system.

There are several ways of identifying the values and beliefs of an organisation:

1. Look at the product line. Is the company producing something that is harmful to the environment or the health of people in general?

2. Look at the espoused values and beliefs of the organisation from its website.

3. Look at the awards and recognitions that it has got.

4. Look at the news items related to the company. What is it in news for?

5. Look at the corporate social responsibility work of the company?

6. Speak to a few people working in the company.

Once you have answers to these questions you will have a fair idea about the values and beliefs that are followed in the company pertaining to society, country, customer and the employees.

Exercise

Write down in the table next page the possible career options that you have in your mind. You might be confused about career options if you think that your professional qualification lends you just one type of a career. However, don't forget that even same professional qualification can make you end up in two very opposite types of careers. For example, an Electrical engineer can choose to be a Plant Maintenance Engineer, Design Engineer, Software Engineer, Consultant, or may even decide to go for higher studies. Think over the possible career options that you have depending on your professional qualification or your interests. Take help from others. You may also go through job portals to see what types of opportunities exist for your professional qualifications. Against each option write the name of a successful person that you know in that particular career (in case you know none, use technology. Linkedin might be a great resource in such exploration). Try to get answers to the following questions from him:

1. What are some of the personality traits that are required to be successful in that career?

2. What type of knowledge, skills and abilities are required to be successful in that career?

Now based on the answers to these questions and your score in RIASEC model, your Multiple Intelligence type and the skills and knowledge that you have, try to find out the fit and gaps between what you aspire to be and what you actually are currently. Write down your actions steps to fill the gap in the last column.

Table 2.3

S. No.	Career Option	Name of a successful person in the career	Characteristics of the Career in terms of Personality Traits, Knowledge, Skills & Abilities.	Your RIASEC Type (your best guess)	Your Multiple Intelligence Type	Your repertoire of Knowledge and skills	Do you have it in you?	What would you do to fill the gap?

How do I do what I do best?

While the last four questions dealt with your innate and acquired characteristics and traits the questions that follow now will deal with your style of working. A consciousness about your styles helps you improve your effectiveness at work. It will help you organise your work in the best possible way. If you are still in student life this awareness will help you prepare well for your exams and placement process.

In an article *Managing Oneself*[8], Peter Drucker suggested asking a series of questions on understanding yourself. I have adapted those questions to deal with our questions here. I am taking four main questions here:

How do I learn?

Human brains are learning machines. Even without conscious effort we keep on learning about the world around us and about ourselves. In fact all of us are 'intuitive scientists' who keep coming up with hypotheses about how things work. I remember as a child I had a hypotheses that wind blew because of the movement of trees. It was only later that I learnt that it was actually the other way round. My theory about wind now appears very absurd and naïve in hindsight.

David Kolb came up with the idea that we all learn like this – from experience. Left to ourselves, we have only one way to learn – *experiential learning*[9]. We go through experiences, look at our experiences, come up with abstract concepts and then experiment those concepts to test their validity. The experiments lead to further experiences spinning off next learning cycle. We may start at any of the four points – Experience, Observation, Conceptualisation, and Experimentation – to move on and keep refining our concepts.

Albeit all the four steps in the learning cycle are important for learning to complete, we have our preferences to learn through one or two of these steps. This preference of ours defines our learning style. Because we have a preference for a particular style the chances of learning increases if we start our learning cycle from that particular style and progressively move to other styles.

Besides these styles we also have our own preferences for learning through any of these three modes:

    I. **Visually:** By looking at pictures, graphical representations, colour schemes or even reading.

    II. **Auditory:** By listening to others speaking about something.

    III. **Kinesthetically:** By actually doing the thing ourselves.

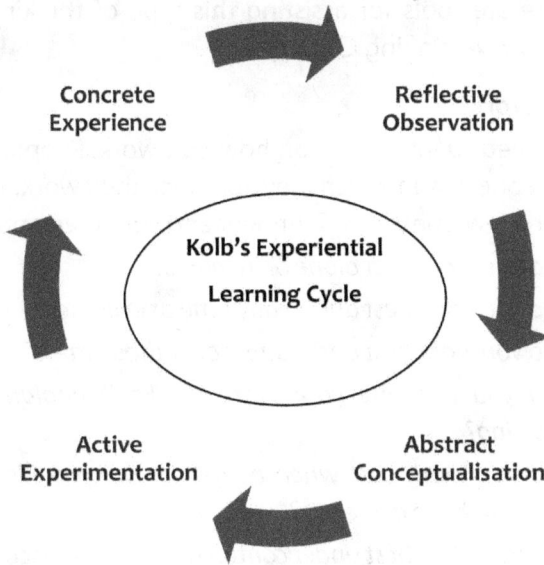

Concrete
Experience

Reflective
Observation

Kolb's Experiential

Learning Cycle

Active
Experimentation

Abstract
Conceptualisation

Figure 2.3

There are online tests available for learning styles also. You may like to take them for identifying your learning style.

How do I think?

Any work requires us to think; thinking about solutions to the problems, about planning, about others, and about ourselves. Thinking is a primary job in the knowledge economy we are living in. There are two ways of thinking: **Linear thinking** – It is a sort of logical thinking in which you move in a sequential manner from one argument or logic to another. This type of thinking is utilised in solving technical or mathematical problems. There even are analytical tools for this approach of thinking – Fishbone Diagram, Why-why Analysis, Statistical Analysis, etc. **Associative thinking** – It is also called lateral thinking. In this type of thinking you jump from one idea to another associated idea which might not be logically or conspicuously linked to the first one. It is used for solving problems in a novel or creative way. There are tools for assisting this type of thinking also – *Mind* Maps, Six Thinking Caps, etc.

How do I work?

You also need to introspect on how you work. People differ in more than one way in which they approach their work. You need to answer a few questions to understand your own approach:

- ✓ *Do you work best alone or in teams?*
- ✓ *Do you work best during day time or evenings?*
- ✓ *Do you work best under stress or without stress?*
- ✓ *Do you organise your work or like it unplanned and flowing?*
- ✓ *Do you work best when guidelines are provided or you want to have a free say?*
- ✓ *Do you work best under control or without any control?*

Try to find out the answers to these questions from your own experiences in your college or school.

You may ask these questions during your interview from the interviewer to find out if the profile and the organisation match your profile.

When am I at my best?

Your skills, knowledge and competencies provide you the capability to deliver at your job but they don't ensure that the job would be done in the best possible manner. Kurt Lewin, who is regarded as the father of the field of *"Organisation Behaviour"*, suggested that the behaviour of a person is a function of his own personality and the environment around him. It is expressed like:

$B = f(p \times e);$

Where,

B=Behaviour

p=Personality Characteristics

e= Environment

Also, in addition, humans have different preferences for environmental characteristics that help them deliver to their best potential. So while choosing the job or the organisation, it is a good idea to know what are your own preferences for the environmental characteristics that help you excel in your job. This can actually avoid you getting stuck in an environment that brings out marginal or sub-optimal performance from you. In order to deal with this question you will need to answer three sub-questions:

What motivates me?

David McClelland, an American psychologist, studied what motivates people as they go around living their lives. He said that there are three sources of motivation[10] for people: Achievement, Affiliation, and Power.

People who are motivated by *achievement* seek to excel. They are moderate risk takers. They neither opt for very high risk nor very low. The tasks that they chose for themselves are ones which challenge their skills moderately, going for not too difficult and not too easy challenges. They seek constant feedback to check their progress. Working alone or with other high achievers is their choice of working.

People, who are motivated by *affiliation*, want their work to provide them opportunities to interact and build relationships with others. They feel a need for being accepted. They do well in client interaction or sales profiles.

Power needs in people can be of two types – *Personal* or *Institutional*. People who are motivated through *personal power* want to direct and control others. They often antagonise people. On the other hand, people who feel motivated by *institutional power* use power derived from their official roles to accomplish organisational objectives.

What culture fits me best?

Organisations have a relatively stable set of values, beliefs, assumptions, mores that help them take decisions. This set is called culture. Different types of people find it easier to adapt to different types of cultures. You need to understand your preference to guide your own selection of organisations.

We will discuss more about culture in **chapter no. 10**

What size of organisation do I deliver best in?

Organisations come in various shapes and sizes. Smaller organisations are more informal but centralised than the bigger organisations. But, they are many times faster in decision making due to their smaller size and lesser bureaucracy. There are other differences also like career growth, career opportunities, and cultural diversity that a difference in size of the organisation implies.

We will learn more about organisations in chapter 10.

What are my success criteria?

A job or a career is meaningless if it doesn't result in a feeling of success. But success might mean two different things to two different people. In fact, if you go on asking people their personal definition of success, they will probably have different words explaining it.

Laura Nash and Howard Stevenson also studied the concept of success and tried to see if there is any similarity in the way people see success. They published their findings in an article[11] published in Harvard Business Review - "*Success that lasts*". Laura Nash and Howard Stevenson proposed that enduring success has four irreducible components.

1. **Happiness** – Feelings of pleasure or contentment about your life.
2. **Achievement** – Accomplishments that compare favourably against similar goals that others have strived for.
3. **Significance** – The sense that you have made a positive impact on the people you care about.
4. **Legacy** – A way to establish your values or accomplishments to help others achieve future success.

You might like to define your success criteria against each of these four components.

Table 2.4

S. No.	Success Component	Success Criterion
1	What defines happiness for you in a job?	
2	What are the accomplishments you want to achieve towards the end of your career life?	
3	How would you make a positive impact on the people you care about?	
4	What would you like to be remembered as in terms of your values and accomplishments?	

Conclusion

The job of finding a job begins with knowing oneself. The question *"Who am I?"* can be broken down into four constituent questions – *"What do I bring to work?", "How do I do what I do best?", "When do I do my best?"*, and *"What are my success criteria?"*.

Every individual brings their personality traits, intelligence, skills and knowledge, and values and beliefs to work. This bag of goodies has to match with the requirements of the job for happiness and satisfaction of the job-holder and quality of the job done.

People also have different styles of working. They have different styles of learning and thinking and accomplishing tasks. Self-awareness of one's style helps him optimise his effectiveness at work.

The environment in which a person works also does have effect on the quality and effectiveness of the work a person does. People have different propensities for work environment.

Some people like to work in a smaller organisation others in a big one. Some people like structured environment and others flexible. Organisations also differ in their culture. You may be more successful in a particular culture than another because of the fit between your values, beliefs and assumptions with the organisation.

No career is complete without the achievement of success. Success, according to Laura and Stevenson, has four irreducible components – Happiness, Achievement, Significance, and Legacy. You must try to define your success criteria with these four components in mind.

Out in the Battle field

Going through the recruitment process is as much about confidence and self-belief as about a diligent preparation. Understanding what recruiters look for, what criteria assessments tests and group discussions assess you on, what answers interviewers expect to their questions, and what foibles the interviewers are prone to, can help you perform to your best potential during the recruitment process by enhancing your belief in yourself.

CHAPTER 3

Who Do Companies Scout For?

Answering the question "Who do companies scout for?" requires us to understand another fundamental question – "Why do companies go for campus recruitments at all?"

Any organisation needs people to function. There are different sources of people coming from – they may come from other companies, from within the company through promotions or job rotation, or from campuses. Employees sourced through the first two sources have an advantage – they come with a readily available set of skills and knowledge. They can start performing from the very next day. However, they also come with some limitations:

- They come with conditioned minds. They have been in the profession for several years, thus it is difficult for them to change themselves; to learn new things; and, create new things.
- They come at a premium. Hiring new people means giving them salary hike for the same work that they are doing in their current jobs.
- The people coming from other organisations also come with their cultural baggage and it becomes difficult sometimes for them to adapt to the change.

Smaller and mid-level companies tend to rely only on the first two sources. They need people who could come and start performing immediately. They can't afford to spend money on training people who are not immediately productive. It is the big, established, growth-oriented companies which decide to hire fresh blood to rejuvenate their organisations. This stream is critical to sustain the growth that these companies envisage for themselves. Fresh, young people are supposed to bring in new ideas uncontaminated with old, traditional, run-of-the-mill thinking. These people are looked upon as potentials for future leadership positions. It is easy to train them, mould them to suit the requirements of a rapidly growing business. They come with a lot of enthusiasm and intrinsic motivation and zeal to prove themselves. People who come through this stream grow up to fill the mid-level management positions of the company and create a robust leadership pipeline.

What are the traits that the recruiters look for in a fresher?

The companies, as we just discussed, need freshers to bring in fresh ideas, creativity, and a robust leadership pipeline for the organisation. In order to fulfill these objectives most companies have a fair idea of what traits they look for in the prospective trainees. Some companies even train their interviewers to assess the applicants on the established criteria.

In this chapter, we will deal with the traits that most organisations find desirable in the candidates that they select.

Ability to learn fast

Recruiters coming to campuses look for people who have the potential to learn quickly. It is because a lot of investment is made in training young professionals who join the organisation directly from campuses. In order to justify this investment the recruited candidates must have the ability to pick up new knowledge and skills in as less a time as possible. They look for attributes like working memory, inductive reasoning, deductive reasoning, etc. These attributes are part of "Fluid" Intelligence which defines the ability of a person to solve problems and identify solutions in fresh and novel ways. It also helps the individual acquire knowledge of facts, processes and procedures.

There are different ways in which organisations measure fluid intelligence of the candidates: through aptitude tests, through problem solving exercises, and through interviewing. Some aptitude tests are designed to measure your fluid intelligence through your performance on attributes like perceptual ability, working memory, numerical accuracy and speed, reasoning, and spatial and visual ability. These tests are timed and scores are often compared with global database to arrive at the final quotient or score.

Psychologists now are of the view that it is possible to improve fluid intelligence by regular and consistent practice. In an article published in 2008 in a popular magazine called "Wired", the author discussed the experiments conducted by scientists showing that with about 25 minutes of rigorous mental training a day, healthy adults could improve their mental capacities[1]. The article discussed about a test called *n-back test* which could be one such possible training tool. In n-back test the test-taker is supposed to identify a letter that repeats itself after a gap of 'n' letters in a sequence of letters. For example, in a n-back test, the test-taker will have to identify the emboldened letters given below:

D E J I L **JM** P Q **ML** P T W **P**

The n-back test is available for free on various websites. You may search it yourself on any search engine on the internet.

Ability to think fresh[2]

One important reason, that organisation, recruit young and fresh professionals from campuses, is the fresh ideas, which they generally could come with. Fresh ideas require ability to think creatively, without any prejudice or preconceived notions.

The recruiters often provide candidates with hypothetical situations and then ask them to suggest a solution. The novel, creative, and off-beat solutions are the ones that the recruiters often expect for such situations. Sometimes they also present a riddle or a puzzle before you which need lateral thinking for solving that. An example is:

What is HIJKLMNO?

The usual answers are letters of English alphabet, some code language, etc. But the most creative answer to this is "water". Try to guess how. (H to O)

Ability to think fresh also involves ability to come out of our cognitive-miserness. Part of our brain, which is responsible for holding working memory for solving problems consciously, is very miser. It is because problem solving is an energy intensive process. We have evolved to avoid thinking as long as it is not very essential. That is why we have problem-solving-strategies that depend on old experiences, heuristics, and patterns. However, there is a great danger of missing out on right solution if we adopt these strategies. Consider the example given below:

Married or Unmarried
John is looking at Linda and Linda is looking at George.
John is married and George is Unmarried.
Is a married person looking at an unmarried person?
a) Yes
b) No
c) Can't be determined

If you are like most people your answer would be "c". It seems obvious that when we don't know the marital status of Linda we can't come to any conclusion.

But, the right answer is 'a'.

Here, the trap is our reluctance to look at the problem from all sides. The right way of solving this puzzle is to make assumptions about Linda's marital status and then look at the veracity of the statement. Suppose Linda is married. In this case, Linda, who is married, is looking at George who is unmarried. So, the statement is true. Suppose Linda is unmarried. In that case John, who is married, is looking at Linda, who is unmarried. So again the statement is true.

Try to find out and solve as many problems as possible for performing well on this part of the selection process. Our brain learns intrinsically and unconsciously through experience to learn new strategies and use them as default when the repeat situations are encountered. Solving more and more problems using lateral thinking will help you make lateral thinking one of the preferred strategies for your brain.

Good communication skills

I still remember a mail that I once got from a student of an Engineering Institute. In the mail he requested me to allow him and his other batchmates to do some projects in my organization as part of their curriculum. I could not hold my laughter after reading that mail. The mail went like this:

Respected Sir,

We, XYZ College of Engg. & Tech, Hyderabad, Civil Engg. Dept. has requested to you that we do as a project work (as construction/highway/irrigation/flyovers etc.,) In iv b. Tech as a part of curriculum.

We would like to requested to you is please give us one chance for me ,for doing of your valuable projects in specified fields as above. Please inform me .....Reg.....

Thank you Sir,

Students,

Dept.Of Civil Engg Section,

It is appalling to see the poor standard of English usage by a student who is supposed to become a qualified engineer in a few months.

A good command over language and the ability to communicate fluently can take you very far. If I say that communication skills can overshadow most of your flaws in the interview process, it will not be a hyperbole. The interviewer knows only as much and as well about you as you tell him. Though it is not always true but many interviewers take communication skills as a proxy for other important skills required for the job. This effect is called 'Halo Effect'. This is not fair! You might complain that it is not fair, but, that's how it is! Good communication skills are also preferred because there is no job that could be accomplished without communicating with others in one form or the other. Communication skills include not only the verbal part but also the non-verbal part. Your body language, your facial expressions, your tone, pitch, etc., all go in making you a master communicator.

It is a sad fact that many of our brilliant engineers passing out of engineering institutes are ill-equipped with this important competency. In fact many engineers demonstrate intellectual arrogance by downplaying the importance of soft-skills including communication. By the time they realise the truth, it is usually too late, and they find themselves struggling at the bottom rungs of the organisational ladder.

Communication skills are assessed during campus recruitments through a variety of tools and techniques. Companies use combination of written tests, group discussions, presentations, etc., to assess candidate's grasp over communication skills. We will learn more about how to develop communication skills in the chapter – "Getting through interviews".

Enterprising attitude

Einstein said, "No problem can be solved from the same level of thinking that created it." And, that's particularly why companies look for people who don't think at the current level in the organisation but at an altogether different level. Enterprising attitude means solving problems creatively, taking calculated risks and persisting till the change is made.

Enterprising attitude does not only mean starting up new companies but also revitalising the existing ones. According to Peter Drucker, "Most of what you hear about entrepreneurship is all wrong. It is not magic; it is not mysterious; and has nothing to do with genes. It is a discipline and, like any discipline, it can be learned."

The constituents of enterprising attitude are:

○ Ability to find out opportunities for improvement
○ Ability to think new alternatives to problems
○ Courage to take calculated risks
○ Strength to persevere against odds
○ Tolerance for uncertainties and ambiguities

As a Management Trainee, I once complained to my boss that there were many problems in the organisation. He replied saying that it was the exact reason that I was recruited. It is easy for people to point out problems in the organisation. Companies need people who can take charge and solve those problems.

The only way recruiters could assess your ability in this trait is through asking questions pertaining to your experience with solving problems during your studies. Involvement in extra-curricular activities might also be considered by some recruiters as a predictor of this ability.

Adaptability

During campus recruitments I find many otherwise promising candidates being rejected because they openly admit that they would not be willing to relocate outside a particular city or wouldn't be ready to work in shifts. Though it is *ok* to be clear in the beginning about what is that you like or don't like to do, such constraints in long term can thwart a career. The business of running a *Business* is a tough business. Businesses work in volatile situations where the state of things changes overnight. People might have to undertake unexpected travel, transfers, or tasks. It requires them to make a lot of compromises. They might have to stay in far-flung towns, do graveyard shift, spend hours every day beyond the stipulated time to complete assignments, work with people from different ethnicities, language, religion, and beliefs.

Working in a company, contrary to some analogies, can never be like working at home. Home is a place where you can do what you like. At work you have to do what the work demands. The best it can get is to get a job that you love to do. Any organisation would like you to adapt to its requirements. Especially in the beginning of the career when you don't have familial responsibilities, companies would like you to stretch and adapt.

While some companies ask direct questions to find out your openness to change, others depend on taking clues from your resume – How many cities you have lived in? How many schools you went to? Did you reside in a hostel or at home? How many languages could you speak? Some companies might ask you to respond to a psychometric questionnaire to gauge this trait.

Adaptability is a trait which is valued very highly by all organisations in today's world.

Clarity of goals in life

What is that you want to do in life? It is a tough question, but, very important. Companies want to ensure that you are clear about what your career goals and aspirations are. This is because it gives them a certainty that your and the organisation's goals would be aligned. Though they know that a goal that seems clear to you currently might change later on, it still is a good predictor of the direction that you wish to take in your career.

According to McClelland, a renowned psychologist, achieve-ment orientation is one of the most important competencies that high performers demonstrate. And, all achievement oriented people set goals for themselves. Goal clarity in students thus becomes a predictor of high performance. Goal clarity is more important for success than role-clarity which many job-seekers value more.

Interviewers usually ask the following questions to assess how clear you are about your career goals:

○ Why did you choose to do this particular course?

○ Why did you select this institute?

○ Why do you want to join our company?

○ What are your career plans?

○ Where do you see yourself in five years down the line?

Self-awareness

One of the favourite questions of interviewers is: "What are your strengths and weaknesses?" Many interviewers ask this question to understand how well you know yourself, and some because it is in vogue. Self-awareness is an important trait of successful individuals. It includes, besides the knowledge of strengths and weaknesses, awareness of your motives, desires, aspirations, goals, styles, emotions. Chapter 2 exclusively dealt with this subject. You may refer it again to understand the importance that this particular trait has when it comes to building a career.

Team skills

Most of the work in organisations is accomplished in teams. Thus, it is obviously one of the major traits that companies would prefer to have in the new recruits. Teamwork needs one to rise above individual losses and gains and look at the bigger goal. A good team-player is supposed to understand his role in the bigger perspective, collaborate with others, resolve intra-team conflicts and help the team achieve its goals. In order to assess your abilities to work in a team, recruiters often ask for examples in your life where you could successfully work in teams and demonstrate those skills. Psychometric tools are also used for assessing team skills.

Integrity and Fitment with organisational values and beliefs

If there is one trait that is invariably found among all high performers, it is Integrity. People, who are integral, have a well-defined and relatively stable value system. They would do what it takes to be right and not what it takes to win. Organisations value such people very highly. In fact most big and successful organisations continually observe if their people get results at the cost of their values and beliefs. Such people don't last long in the organisations and are asked to leave even if it means monetary and resource loss to the company.

Organisations are socio-technical systems. Each organisation is idiosyncratic in its culture, language, values, beliefs, assumptions, rituals and mores. When a new employee enters this system he has to work towards aligning his own principles, values, and guiding beliefs to those of the organisation. How effectively he works in an organisation depends on the alignment between his values and beliefs and those of the organisation. If there is a synchrony between the two – the new employee will be able to smoothly sail through the organisation terrain. But in an unfortunate case where these two go counter to each other, it would be really difficult for the person to even take a step further.

This part is very difficult for an interviewer to gauge. They usually lean on behavioural event interviewing and psychometrics to ascertain degree of alignment in the candidate's and the organisation's values and beliefs.

Write down a development Plan

Now that you have gone through the list of traits that companies look for in fresh recruits, you need to draw out a development plan for yourself. Before drawing any development plans it is required that you realise where you stand currently. Without understanding the current reality it might be very difficult to realise change goals. Prepare a feedback form using any online application to develop or upload survey forms. Ask the respondents to rate you on each of the 8 traits (you can't rate yourself on fitment with values and beliefs of all organisations) on a scale of 1-5 (1 being lowest and 5 the highest score). You should carefully select respondents. These could be your friends, classmates, college seniors, teachers, family members or project guides from companies where you did your internship. More respondents you select better are the chances that the feedback is correct. Give more weight to scores received from college seniors, teachers and project guides. Once you have the scores from all these respondents, collate the scores and identify the areas for development and also identify ways to improve on those areas. Use the format below for developing your plan.

Table 3.1

Development Plan Format

S. No.	Trait	Current Level based on feedback	Desired Level	Actions to be taken	Target Date
1	Ability to learn fast				
2	Ability to think fresh				
3	Communication Skills				
4	Enterprising Attitude				
5	Adaptability				
6	Clarity of Goals				
7	Self Awareness				
8	Team Skills				

Conclusion

Companies look out for fresh and young talent which can provide fresh ideas for revitalising the company. They look for people who can learn fast, think fresh, communicate fluently, show enterprising attitude, adapt to changes, have clear goals, are self-aware and could perform in teams. Companies also need people who can gel with the culture of their organisation and whose values and beliefs also align. Recruiters use several tools and techniques to assess these traits like – Specific interview questions, Group Discussions, Written Tests, Presentations, and Psychometric Tests. An understanding of the intention behind each of these tools can help a student prepare better for the assessment process.

CHAPTER 4

Mastering Assessment Tests & Group Discussion

"Rising up to the occasion" is one ability that distinguishes high achievers from the average others. In a study (Brian Rogers et al.) it was established that this ability, called *critical ability*, is positively related to career growth and success[1]. Critical ability helps a person to deliver when it matters the most, in a situation where others might choke and flounder under pressure. Performance in Assessment Tests, Group Discussions and Interviews is a lot about critical ability, provided you have other competencies that are required to clear these access controlled gateways to success. Brian Rogers believes that critical ability can be developed through concerted practice.

Before we start discussing how to master assessment test and group discussions, I would like to underscore the fact that there is no shortcut to success. Your performance in assessment tests and Group Discussions can't be better than you are. Provided that the maximum number of candidates is screened out in these two steps alone, the purpose of this chapter is to sensitise you to costly mistakes you may avoid and simple techniques you may adopt to perform most optimally in this part of the recruitment process.

Why Assessment Tests and Group Discussions?

When companies visit campuses for recruitment they are often flooded with a number of applications. Just imagine the plight of the interviewers if they were to interview just about anyone who was interested in the job. Thus, they put the applicants through a process consisting of several rounds to eliminate students who lack basic requirements of the job. They usually put the candidates through – Technical Tests, Aptitude Tests, Group Discussions, and Personal Interviews. There is one fundamental difference between assessment tests, GD on one hand and personal interviews on the other. The former two are tools for rejection and the latter is a tool for selection. Thus assessment tests and GD are more impersonal and ruthless than interviews. Assessment tests are designed to throw-up the best out of the lot on the basis of their technical knowledge and aptitude. Since the numbers are usually still high, GDs are conducted to eliminate people who lack communication skills. Together – Assessment Tests and GDs – relieve the recruiters from a lot of effort.

Don't confuse assessment tests referred to here with psychometric tests. Psychometric tests are not used for rejecting candidates. They are putatively used to help the recruiters fit eligible candidates in suitable roles. However, the truth is that in most companies psychometric tests are safely tucked away in the personal files of the selected candidates and they are never referred to again. The tests are administered just to ensure compliance with the established process.

ASSESSMENT TESTS

What Do Assessment Tests Assess?

Assessment Tests are generally of two types – Technical and Aptitude. Technical tests, as the name suggests, aim at testing the technical expertise of the candidates. These tests are generally of medium difficulty level. The second type of test called Aptitude test is either done in conjunction with the technical test or sometimes as the next level of screening. These tests are designed to assess the aptitude of the candidates for the type of job being offered by the company. As most of the managerial and engineering jobs require verbal, critical reasoning, numerical abilities for winning performance, most of the aptitude tests are designed to measure those constructs.

(Aptitude tests for some niche jobs might be very different from this. We are restricting our discussion here to Engineering or Management Graduates only).

Who designs Assessment Tests?

Many companies use standard tests which are scientifically validated and are used globally. The advantage of using these tests is the reliability of the test results. Other companies develop their own tests and then establish norms based on repeated use of the tests in campuses. In any case, these tests are usually very objective, relevant, and effective in screening out students who would not otherwise be able to clear the interview process.

How do Recruiters Make Their Decision Based on Assessment Tests?

Assessment Tests as we discussed are supposed to screen in the best candidates for interview. Though companies usually have a minimum passing percentage, many companies make a merit list and shortlist only the top quartile for the further rounds. The percentage of selected students though might differ from one company to another. The basic idea of administering these tests is to reject those candidates who have less chance of making it through the final interview thereby reducing the burden on the interviewers and making the process more efficient and fast.

Some companies also compare the relative performance at different campuses and decide on different passing percentage for different institutes. However in such cases they also decide to pay the students differentially.

Exhibit 4.1

Amazing Facts About Your Brain

1. Brain uses more than 20% of the energy consumed by your body. This is more than any other organ in the body.

2. Pre-frontal Cortex (PFC), which is the centre for planning, making decisions, working memory and conscious thinking in your brain has limited capability, consumes a lot of energy and gets tired easily.

3. PFC can effectively and efficiently tackle only one attentive task at a time.

4. New neurons keep on getting generated throughout your life. If you don't use them through new learning, they die.

5. Brain is very plastic and can be trained to increase general intelligence

How to score high in Assessment Tests?

Nothing can replace a genuine, sincere, and concerted hardwork in understanding the fundamentals of your course subjects in preparation for assessment tests.

However, besides preparation, you might also increase your score by doing a few extra things just before or during the test.

First thing that is pretty obvious and I know that you would do even if no one tells you to do it is to find out the pattern of assessment tests for different companies from your seniors, friends in other institutes, and internet. Once you have the pattern of the test and you know which company you want to target, you should prepare accordingly.

Second important thing is to avoid sleep deprivation. The anxiety of appearing for the recruitment process in your dream company can be a source of lot of anxiety. This anxiety might keep you stay awake the previous night. Any amount of preparation might appear insufficient and you might find yourself going through your books again, the whole night, just to ensure that you don't miss out any question that the interviewer might ask. However, this is exactly what you should not do. Don't stay awake the night before the test. It has been proved that partial sleep deprivation (less than 7hrs in 24 hrs) can impair executive functions of the brain. Ability to manipulate information to arrive at a logical result is also one of the several executive functions of the brain – which can be impaired by lack of sleep. Also remember, a relaxed mind is a more effective and efficient mind.

Third thing that you should not take lightly is your breakfast. When the judgment day finally arrives, you might find yourself in a hurry. But, ensure that in this hurry you don't skip breakfast. There has been much research on the effect of skipping breakfast on cognitive performance of students and adults. It has been found that both adults and children perform better in memory and recall tests when they had a proper breakfast. Recollection speed, which is the key to performing at assessment tests, is also enhanced by having a good and healthy breakfast. So all those claims that students who have regular breakfast perform better in their studies are not hoax; they are real[2].

The fourth piece of advice would be to help you prepare yourself for handling anxiety. Having breakfast gives your brain enough energy to control your anxiety level. But anxiety is not an easy thing to handle. Even the best of the bests have anxieties that might lower their performance during the selection process. And, it is necessary that you deal with this anxiety and don't let it interfere with your performance. One technique that you could adopt for dealing with pre-exam anxiety is writing down your worries on a piece of paper just before the exam. Recent studies[3] by psychologists at the University of Chicago showed that students who actually wrote down their worries for ten minutes on a piece of paper before the exam performed much better than those who did not. So why don't you also follow the same technique to rein in your anxieties.

The brain is an energy guzzler which doesn't store its energy. It runs on pure glucose, which it takes from the blood directly. Brain consumes more than 20% of the total energy consumed by the entire body, more than any other organ. The consumption increases further when you do a cognitive task such as understanding or solving a problem. This is one important reason that you should not skip breakfast in general and in specific before an exam. Further, though I wouldn't suggest this to Diabetic patients, a glucose drink just before may improve your score on both technical and aptitude tests.

The final suggestion that I have for you is to leverage knowledge of brain functioning to boost your performance in assessment tests and GD. The Pre-frontal Cortex in the human brain is the center of all executive functions including planning, self-control, conscious thinking and working memory. This part is less than 4% by volume of the entire brain. It is very limited in its scope and can get tired soon. Cognitive tasks deplete the blood glucose available for brain quickly. Based on these facts you may rightly say that the proponents of multitasking are wrong. Our brains perform best when attentively working on just one thing. If there are several tasks or thoughts vying for our attention, the effectiveness of the brain comes down dramatically. In fact that is the exact reason why just one worrying thought is enough to make you choke under pressure situations. That worrisome thought divides your attention and distracts you from the immediate task at hand. Practising mindful awareness can help you improve your attention paying capability and can improve your performance at cognitive tasks. You may start mindful awareness training by doing simple things like observing your breath for 2-3 minutes in the morning, before lunch, before dinner, and before going to bed. You may also try other exercises – try to observe your heartbeat when you have just ran on tread-mill, try to feel the air in your hair while riding your motorbike, feel the taste of the food consciously while you eat and so on. If you have practised enough, during the test you can bring all your attention first to the present through focusing on your breath and then transfer that focus to the task at hand. And, as you know once your focus is only at the task at hand, your efficiency and effectiveness both improve remarkably.

There is one more advice derived from the way the brain functions – attempt the easier questions first. Attempting tougher questions first may deplete your brain glucose level in the very beginning. It might further result in reduced accuracy with even the easier questions.

GROUP DISCUSSION

What is Group Discussion and why is it used?

Group Discussion (GD) is a methodology for observing communication and leadership skills of individuals in an impromptu, ambiguous and leaderless situation. Recruiters use GD as a tool for rejecting candidates who don't possess the required level of communication and interpersonal skills. The candidates who make it through the GD are usually not differentiated on the basis of their performance in GD. Therefore it is rather a rejection tool than a selection tool.

In GD the recruiters ask the candidates to sit together in a group of 5-10 and then ask them to discuss on a particular topic. The topics could be either in a debate format (for or against positions) or explorative format (open-ended and non-judgmental). The students are often provided some time (2-5 minutes) to prepare for the discussion. The duration of GD could be 10-15 minutes and is rarely beyond that. The recruiters keenly observe the candidates as they discuss on the topic provided and make notes based on a pre-decided criteria. The criteria used often are:

1. Ability to articulate and convey ideas
2. Assertiveness and ability to influence others
3. Leadership skills
4. General knowledge
5. Listening skill

How to prepare and perform well in GDs?

A good performance in GDs requires intensive practice. GDs are characterised by short time for preparation, even shorter time for making your point and often hostile competition (Sometimes GDs even turn very ugly). It is because of these characteristics some people warn that GDs might actually sometimes eliminate candidates who are good otherwise but can't force them through chaos existing at the time of GD. To eliminate this error, recruiters often provide one minute to each participant towards the end to share his/her views with the rest of the group. Whatever be the efficacy and validity of the method, almost all companies have GD as an integral part of their campus recruitment process, so it is better to be ready to face it rather than question it and find excuses for not being able to make through it.

I would discuss now with you how to prepare for each of the criterion that the recruiters look for while you participate in GD. The preparation will be long and would need concerted effort from your side to yield results.

Ability to articulate and convey ideas

All of us have thoughts and opinions about most of the things around us, but not all of us can speak those ideas out in a way that the other person understands it the way we mean it. It is because thoughts and opinions in our heads are often abstract and vague. The art of converting those vague and abstract thoughts and opinions into words and sentences is called Articulation (In a strict sense, 'articulation' in speech means the way we use our mouth, throat, lungs, and tongue to create sound).

You may do an exercise to check your ability to articulate the abstract. Take a picture with a rich background – a market place, a museum, bus-stop, railway station, people celebrating a festival etc. – and try to explain the picture to a friend of yours. After explaining, show the picture to him/her. Ask how close your explanation was to the picture. His/her answer will indicate the degree of articulation that you demonstrated in this exercise. You may keep practising this exercise to improve your articulation ability.

In a GD the participants are supposed to discuss with others their ideas about the topic provided to the group. The topic provided for GD could be anything related to current affairs – Sports, Movies, Controversies, Politics; or Social Phenomena – Social Communities, Poverty, Discrimination, Diversity; or Business – Global Trends, Corporate Social Responsibility; or just random topics – Red, Umbrella, Zipper, Monkey, or any other weird topic.

Needless to say, the first thing that you need to speak is 'Ideas'. For if you don't have ideas the question of articulation doesn't arise. GD might be simpler, for obvious reasons, for candidates who keep a tab on current affairs through news-papers, magazines or TV. It is also simpler for people who have a regular reading habit. However, looking at the range of topics that might come up for the discussion, it is difficult to be perfectly ready for every topic. Depending on the topic provided you have to make do with whatever information you have and deliver your best.

Most topics can be prepared through a habit of regular reading of newspapers. Track latest developments in politics, sports, movies, international arena, controversies, scams, etc. Usually recruiters select the most contemporary topic for GDs. Make a list of probable topics and discuss those issues with your friends and peers. Read blogs and magazines to know opinions of others about those developments. Listen to debates on TV channels. Have an opinion yourself about them. If you don't have an opinion yourself then you might not sound authentic while speaking in the GD. It is *Ok* to quote others but recruiters will certainly be impressed if you have your own reasoned ideas and opinions. A caveat here is – avoid very strong opinions.

There are some techniques below that might help you to get ideas. It is advisable that you practice these techniques in mock GDs with your peers.

1. In GDs participants are supposed to put together their thoughts in 2-5 minutes. Use Mind Mapping technique to put together the key ideas around the main topic. Once you have the key ideas, further branch off them to get associated ideas. (Figure 1). Use associated ideas to frame your point of view on the topic provided.

2. In case you don't know enough on the topic, make sure you are not among the first few to speak. Wait for some time and listen to what others have to say. Use your ingenuity later to put together ideas and speak. Try grouping similar ideas and share what sense it makes with the group.

3. You may start asking a few questions to the group. It might appear to be stupid but you feel that it is wise to discuss some fundamental questions to begin with and then ask a few questions. It will help you to get some ideas as well as establish yourself as one of the moderators also.

Having ideas gives you some stuff to speak. Speaking, however, is entirely different from thinking and ideating. According to a survey conducted in the United States public speaking is one of the biggest fears in an average American. It scores higher than being bitten by a dog. Such a survey is yet to be done in India but I doubt if Indians will fare any better. Provided that English is the second language for us, fear of speaking might be even more. Main challenges that most students suffer from are – poor grammatical constructions, poor vocabulary, usage of complex and convoluted sentences, usage of difficult words, slow or fast pace, Mother Tongue Influence, and Stammering.

Overcoming these obstacles requires the will to learn, concerted practice, and regular feedback.

Mastering grammar is essential for speaking any language effectively. Poor grammatical usage leaves a very bad impression on the recruiters. Master your Articles, Tenses, and Subject-Verb Agreement, if nothing else. You don't really need to learn the definitions of different parts of speech but some basic rules must be clear. Discussing English Grammar will be out of the scope of this book. So find out a good English Grammar book and start practicing. Remember that the key to mastering grammar is practice. Go to website www.ego4u.com for excellent free material and practice tests on English Grammar.

Speaking is all about words. A strong vocabulary is a prerequisite for excelling in GDs. It helps you convey abstract ideas in a more concrete manner and at the same time conveys to the recruiter that the speaker is well-read and thoughtful. Make reading a habit. Read at least one book per month, besides your course books. Keep making a list of new words that you learn. Try using new words while speaking until you get used to them. Building vocabulary is a long process and you need to start early to build a solid bank of words. Read "Word Power Made Easy" by Norman Lewis.

People tend to use complex and convoluted sentences which confuse the speaker as much as the listeners. Try restricting yourself to using simple sentences. One habit that adds to this problem is using 'and' at the end of each sentence you speak. Because of this, you have a long string of sentences that ultimately ends either inconclusively or incompletely. Try speaking on a topic for a couple of minutes and count how many times you use 'and'. Keep practising until you decrease it to bare minimum.

Using Mind-Map Technique to Generate Ideas

Mind-Map is a technique devised by Tony Buzan for aiding lateral and associative thinking. Mind-Map helps you expand a single idea into a number of associated ideas, classify existing ideas, and generate new ideas. It's quite a useful aid for writing, making decisions, and solving problems.

Mind-Map can be used as a tool for creating ideas around the topic provided for GD. For example the topic provided to you is " Group Discussion as a tool for selection".

Step1. Write the topic in the center of the page.

Step2. Make several branches and write some associated ideas or key questions around the topic – Why GDs? Disadvantages?Advantages?Alternatives?

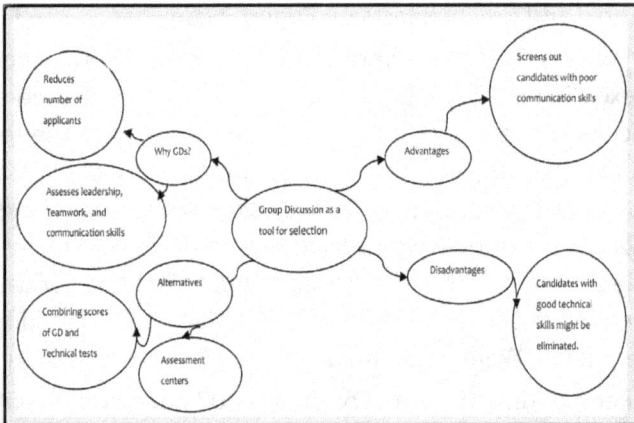

Step3. Expand each of the new nodes with associated ideas or answers as shown

Step4. Try to frame each of the ideas or answers into sentences. See if there is some relationship between ideas that otherwise appear in different branches. For Example – use advantages and disadvantages branches to think about alternatives.

Exhibit 4.2

Why would you like to use a word that people could not understand? You certainly need to make an impression on the recruiters but with difficult words you might fail to put your point across. People who try to showcase their superiority by using difficult words are often disliked. Try using words that people usually know or may understand easily in the context.

Do you speak very fast or very slow? Ask your friends for feedback. If you speak very fast, you might run out of your ideas before others understand you. If you speak too slow people will interrupt you and you might find yourself not being able to complete what you want to say. Try to optimise your pace.

Mother Tongue Influence and Stammering are two difficult problems which certainly require more help than you could provide yourself working alone. These two problems can have a devastating effect not only on GD alone but also on your overall career prospects. Fortunately, both problems can be rectified. You may consider calling on a speech therapist to conquer these challenges.

Assertiveness and ability to influence others

The classic definition of assertiveness is not compromising your rights while respecting others' rights. In GDs, as noted earlier, there is a competitive atmosphere. Everyone wants to speak to make an impression on the recruiters. In such a situation many people find it difficult to speak anything at all. The reason usually is lack of assertiveness. Assertiveness in the context of GD is the ability to say what you want to say and be heard by others. It also implies sounding certain of what you are saying, but, in case somebody else puts up a strong antithesis, gracefully accepting that you were wrong.

People often find it difficult to make themselves heard because of following reasons:

- ☒ Waiting that somebody else will ask for their opinion.
- ☒ Repeatedly saying, "I want to say something", but never actually saying it.

- ☒ Making a point that is very different from what the group is discussing.
- ☒ Trying to interrupt when one participant is addressing question of a particular participant.
- ☒ Speaking very slowly. Using too much of 'er's and 'ah's or pure silence.
- ☒ Using long sentences that take time to put the main idea across.
- ☒ Beating about the bush.
- ☒ Using vague language – 'You know', 'Kind of', 'They say', etc.
- ☒ Not sounding certain of what they are saying. Using no facts and figures. Relying totally on phrases like 'I feel', 'I think', etc.

Decide whether you want to initiate the discussion. Initiate only if you have an idea in mind on how to take the discussion further. Initiation requires you to take the role of the moderator for the rest of the discussion. There are no brownie points for just being the first person to speak. I find many participants initiating the discussion with a few points and then remaining silent for the rest of the discussion. Such behaviour would have a detrimental effect on your chances of clearing this round. Before initiating, make sure that you have something to say that will describe the flow of the discussion further, and then keep moderating the discussion till the end. Further, to make a start and continue it, you should understand that nobody is going to ask you for your opinion. If you have enough ideas, begin by sharing your opinion in a structured fashion. Say what you want to say, say it, and then tell them what you said. If you haven't started the discussion, it is not the end of it. There are some opportunities where you can easily get into the discussion. Say, three or four people have spoken about the same topic and one of your ideas has not been discussed, you may get into the discussion by announcing, "We seem to be missing one important point" and then continuing without waiting for anyone's go-ahead.

If you make a valid point people will look forward to listening more from you. In case all your ideas on a particular key idea or sub-topic are exhausted propose changing the direction of the discussion by declaring, "I feel this is time that we look at some of the....." and then continue with your point. You may also keep on looking for ideas that are directly opposed to your ideas and then address the participant, who you disagree with, and tell him that you have a point that might disprove his assumption. In any case, after making the initial declaration, don't wait for response of other participants, and keep on with your line of argument. Remember the mistakes that we discussed earlier to avoid being interrupted while you speak.

GDs usually end up providing you very short time to influence or change others' opinions, but this doesn't mean that you should not try to. Provide facts, figures and reasons to support what you say. Don't make others feel that a particular statement that you say is true just because you believe and say so. Don't raise your voice when someone contradicts you. Acknowledge the equal probability of other point of views being valid and then put across your point once again. Don't be adamant in case others don't buy your point of view. You may end it by saying that perhaps the time was too short to arrive at any final decision.

Finally, assertiveness is all about how much you respect yourself. Others will listen to you only when you are convinced that others should listen to you. People who don't respect themselves don't get respect from anybody.

Leadership Skills

It is difficult to judge leadership skills of the participants in a 15-20 minutes GD. The recruiters look for attributes which can be taken as proxy for real leadership skills. They look for your ability to moderate the discussion. They try to observe if you –

- ✓ Help provide direction to the discussion at crucial junctures – changing topics, coalescing ideas, reaching conclusions.

✓ Manage conflicts

✓ Make meaningful contributions

Some people have an innate ability to do all these things, others need to develop them. And, developing leadership skills is a long process. In case you are not absolutely confident of taking the role of the moderator, it is advisable to avoid. If you set your priorities right, you can still make it through without being a leader.

Ability to listen to others' ideas

An important aspect of communication is the ability to listen actively to others. No surprise that recruiters assess you on this criterion too. Listen actively to what others are saying. It means:Who is saying what? What has been the trajectory of the discussion? Which key ideas have been discussed? Which ideas are similar? Which ideas are dissimilar?

Also note that when you speak

✓ Refer to what others have said. If you could refer names, nothing could beat it

✓ Coalesce ideas and say what you understood from the overall discussion on a particular key idea

✓ Summarise well in the end if asked to do so

You need to keep using your pen and paper throughout the discussion to be able to do so. Use symbols, abbreviations and visual clues to note down the discussion. If you try to write down everything you might lose track of the discussion.

General Knowledge

As recruiters we are often surprised to find that candidates are often not in practice of reading newspapers and are out of contact with even some of the most important developments in business, politics, science, and sports.

Businesses run on information. That is why recruiters look out for people who have a penchant for information. Besides reading newspapers and books, keep a handy note-book in which you may maintain facts, figures and statistics related to various areas. Keep referring to the book often and use the material there during mock discussions (and obviously during the real one). But remember that don't use your knowledge to show-off your superiority. Use knowledge to support your opinion only.

Conclusion

Assessment Tests and GDs are almost universally used for screening applicants for the final interview. The purpose is to eliminate those applicants who are below threshold levels in technical knowledge, aptitude, and communication skills. For getting through these two steps a lot depend on hardwork and sincerity that you put in for preparing well in advance. However, people often fail to perform to their real potential and find themselves screened out much their bemusement. In this chapter you learnt a few techniques and got aware of a few common mistakes that might result in such a sorry end.

World is very unpredictable and so are the requirements that companies may come up with. What we discussed above can be applied to most companies, not all. So be ready for surprises and unexpected patterns in selection process. Remember, ultimately the fortune favours the prepared mind.

CHAPTER 5

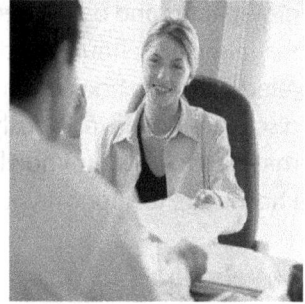

Getting Through Interviews

Personal Interview is an opportunity for the recruiters to interact with the candidates to elicit details that could not be possibly drawn-out in written tests or group discussions. It is also an opportunity for you as a candidate to have undivided attention of the recruiters, to make them see that you are the right fit for the job that they have to offer. And, this also is a window for you to get that information about the company which may help you make a join or not-join decision in case you get the offer. Recruiters often take the selection decision solely on the basis of your performance in the interview and your performance in preceding rounds has little, if any, contribution. We discussed in detail, in chapter-5, the traits that recruiters look for in candidates during campus recruitments. In addition most companies make it clear during the Pre-placement talk, what they would be looking for in the candidates. Most of those traits – universal or specific –become the basis for the questions that would be asked during the interview. The key to success in interviews thus is your ability to provide answers that help the interviewer easily spot those traits in you.

Potential and performance are often correlated but not always. Having potential doesn't necessarily guarantee that interviewers will be able to see that potential and hand-pick you. Showcasing your potential is an art that is innate in some people and which needs to be developed with concerted practice by others. It is unfortunate that many otherwise talented people languish in underpaid jobs because they can't perform well in interviews when they have potential to earn and contribute much more. And, with the notion – *"Past predicts the future"* – which is widely accepted as an axiom in the corporate world, it becomes difficult for these talented people to come out of their sub-optimal positions. Going through interviews is an unnerving process for many and the overwhelming nervousness sometimes proves disastrous for the candidate. Besides nervousness there are several other reasons that we will discuss in this chapter that could result in sub-optimal performance in the interviews. We will also discuss the ways in which a person could best avoid those pitfalls and get a befitting job.

Though interviews are universally used for selection, their validity is not unquestionable. We all know that organisations have people (who are selected through established selection processes, including interview) who perform much below expectations. Such people are live evidence of occasional inefficacy of interview process. That is why I chose to add another interesting aspect here – Interviewers are also human and they are also prone to several biases, stereotypes and other psychological traps. It is important to understand these traps so that you could leverage them to your benefit rather than falling victim to them.

Preparing for interview

The preparation for interviews should start early during your academic course. Most people wait till the final year – when the recruitments begin – to start preparing themselves. It is usually quite late and nothing much could be done in such a short period. There are several steps in preparation that start from building your resume to the point in time when you sit in the chair in front of the interviewers.

Preparing your Resume

An important part of your pursuit for a good job is your Resume. Resume should not be considered as a simple collection of information about you. It is a great tool to find a job if used effectively. The process of building the resume should start early in your academic course. The principles of goal setting can be used to build a great resume. First draft of your resume, early in your course, should be a Future Resume. Write your resume as it should look when you send it to the recruiters. Add what CGPA or Percentage you would have got, what projects you would have done, which competitions you would have won, which events you would have organised, which companies you would have done your internship in, what training programs and certifications you would have, etc. Write your aspirational resume believing that what you write exists in reality. Then use the time you have during your course to make your this resume a reality.

But most people, as noted earlier, write their resume just before the companies start visiting the campus. So we will discuss how to prepare the resume in case you didn't prepare it throughout your academic course. There are several formats for writing resume, and you will get them all over the internet. I will discuss here some of the tips that make an effective resume

- ✓ Do write your career objective as the very first line of the resume. Your career objective should be aspirational, specific, ambitious, but realistic for ex. – To work and develop myself as an expert to be reckoned with in the area of highway designing.
- ✓ Write in detail about the projects and internships that you did as a part of your coursework. Many times interviewers tend to let the entire discussion being driven by the project work alone. Be sure that you can explain the project to the minutest details. Carry the project report along, it provides credibility and can act

86

as a ready reference in case a technical question is asked that requires you to refer numbers and data from the report.

✓ Have a section on technical skills separately. Highlight skills that might interest the recruiter ex. – Advanced Microsoft Excel, Statistical Analysis, Vibration Analysis, Psychometrics, Market Research etc. It will be desirable if you could substantiate your skills in the resume itself with a particular industrial experience or certification.

✓ Have a list of training programs you attended on behavioural or technical skills. If you write a particular program in your list, make sure that you go through the content of the program at least once before coming to the interview.

✓ All other essentials like – Name, date of birth, address, contact number, email id, academic history(reverse chronological order) should be there.

☒ Make sure you don't make any spelling mistakes. All spelling mistakes spell "disaster". Let someone proof-read it for you.

☒ Avoid unprofessional email ids like superhero@anymail. com

☒ Nobody is interested in knowing if you are a bathroom singer or if you like watching Hindi movies. Don't write normal things as your hobbies. To qualify as a hobby a skill requires at least some level of expertise.

☒ Don't write things for which you might not have any proof and which would be inconsequential for the recruiter for ex. – Participated in several debate competitions in school.

The interviewers often depend entirely on your resume to frame questions. Every piece of information in the resume could be used for that purpose. Many times we as interviewers find that the interviewee has just put up a point in the resume which is desirable in a resume but about which the he has no idea. If you are found with such a resume, take it for granted that your interview is over. Authenticity is the key to success in interviews. Your resume should be **100%** authentic.

Preparing answers to general questions

There are some questions that you invariably find face-to-face with in interviews. These general questions are sometimes asked because it is a tradition to ask them and sometimes because the information they provide is indispensable. It is better to prepare and practise extensively answers to these questions in advance.

- *"Tell me something about yourself."* – This is an open ended question in which the interviewer doesn't even specify what he wants to know about you. The best way to answer this question is to divide it in a few sections – Academics, Family Background, Extracurricular activities, Interests – and then answer the question in each of these categories. Avoid making this part too lengthy; ideal duration for this question is 2 minutes. Sometimes a few candidates use this as an opportunity to gain sympathy from the recruiter by explicitly mentioning that they are from a poor background, etc. It is not considered a good sign by most interviewers. Make this part interesting for the interviewer. Highlight important aspects of your personality without sounding boastful. Prepare a note-book in which you write down your achievements and also how you achieved them. Write in it whatever you like about yourself and what others tell is good about you. Keep reading it time and again. It will help you make a self-concept that is easy to put in words.

- *"Why did you choose to take this particular course or college?"* – The interviewer here is trying to understand your decision making process. He wants to see if you take decisions based on what others say or if you have a reasoned decision making process based on your own

88

values and motives in life. The best way to answer this question is to enumerate the options that you had after your school and then provide reasons for not choosing other options. In case you tried other options but failed to realise them – say so. Honesty is the best policy and recruiters are impressed with such frankness.

- *"Where do you see yourself in next 5 years?"* – Remember the point discussed in chapter-4 – One of the main traits that the interviewers look for in the candidates is "Clarity of goals in life". This question lets them find out if you have a long term vision of your career. The answer to this question needs to be answered in a way that sounds neither too ambitious nor too lame. You may answer this question in three parts – learning, achievement and role. Emphasise what you would have learnt in 5 years, what would have been your achievements and what responsibility level (leading a project team, handling a department independently, etc.) you would have reached. Also top-up this question by sharing with them what you would do to achieve it in terms of contributions, training, higher education, etc.

- *"Why do you want to join our company?"* – They want to know if you have done enough homework to know about their company and do you see an alignment between what you want from your career and what they have to offer to you. Answer by elaborating about what you know about the company – its line of business, its growth plans, its people development initiatives – then talk about your career aspirations and show that there is an alignment between the two.

- *"Why should we select you?"* – This is a difficult question. Don't quote your educational qualifications as a reason. Everybody else also has same qualification in your campus. Also, don't start listing general qualities – "I am very hardworking and sincere" for example. Instead you need to tell them that you have everything that they probably would be looking for. Start by saying that you fulfill the basic criteria required for this job but in addition you have done a few extra courses, have a few extra certifications, have been a part of a few relevant projects, etc. You may also pinpoint a few niche skills that are required for the profile that they have to offer and show that you have more than what is required for the job.

- *"What are your strengths and weaknesses?"* – This is a key question and highlights the level of self-awareness you have got. To answer this question you need to make a list of five strengths that you have really demonstrated in your life. The best people to help you in finding this answer are your friends and family members. Ask them what is that they praise in you and also ask them the reasons for why they praise the qualities you have. Practise this answer many times before interviews. The interviewers will expect you to substantiate whatever you say with evidence or incidents. So be prepared for explaining the story. Coming to the weakness part – you should select one weakness that could be improved upon and that would not sound detrimental to your ability to perform in an organisation. Always top-up this answer with an action that you are currently taking to develop on your weakness. For example –"My time-management skills were not that good during school days. I used to find it difficult to divide my time optimally between my passion for sports and doing my homework and studies. During college days I worked on it and now have found a sort of balance between the two. There is still some scope for improvement and I am sure that I would be able to make it."

Always remember while preparing answers that most of these answers require you to quote critical incidents (or simply stories) of when you demonstrated a particular trait or solved a particular problem. As any story, prepare yours to have four parts – *Situation* in which you demonstrated that trait; *Task* that you were expected to accomplish; *Actions* that you took; *Results* that you got. Don't miss out on any of these four parts. Your story is not complete without any one of them. The interviewers these days are trained to identify loopholes in the stories that candidates tell. You need to sound authentic with this **STAR (Situation, Task, Action, & Result)** complete.

Mock Interviews

Mock interviews are your opportunity to test the skills that you are going to learn in this book and will help you improve your articulation. There are some educational institutes which offer you this opportunity for a fee. You may, however, find a mock interviewer very near you. It could be your sister, brother, uncle, friend or a teacher you are at good terms with. He should be someone who has a genuine interest in your development. You don't need someone who would do it just for the sake of doing it. Ask for feedback after the interview and work on improvement.

Due diligence

No one can beat the proactive. When your placement office announces the visit of a particular company gather as much information as possible about the company – History, Mission, Vision, Values, Line of Business, Locations, People Practices, Future Plans, etc. The best source of information about the company obviously is its website. But you search for the latest news items about the company as well. Identify who are the competitors of the company, what are the challenges that it has recently faced and might be facing in future, what awards has it won. Also find out the profiles of the people working with the company (Linkedin or other professional network website). It will help you gather some very interesting facts – What are the roles and responsibilities of people working there? What type of educational qualification do high-fliers have? How is the demography? All this data will help you prepare yourself better to handle specific questions that might be asked during the interview.

Table 5.1

S. No.	Data	Type of questions it may help in
1	What are the roles and responsibilities of people at the company?	Where do you see yourself in 5 years? Why should we select you? Technical Questions
2	What are the qualifications and achievements of high-fliers in the organisation?	How would you develop yourself further after joining the company? Where do you see yourself in 5 years? How would you differentiate yourself from your peers?
3	Locations of business units	Do you have any location preference? (Don't say 'yes' to this answer. Say that you have a preference but that is not a constraint.)
4	All other data	What do you know about our company? Why do you want to join our company? Why should we select you? What do you know about our company?

Grooming

Your first impression is very important. Humans have a tendency to make opinions and evaluate others through their appearance.

Recruiters come to the campus to hire professionals and thus it is very important to look like one. Very recently, I visited the campus of a very reputed Engineering Institute for recruiting Graduate Engineer Trainees. During the pre-placement talk, I was appalled to notice that most of the students had come in casuals (that too shabby), were unshaven, and didn't bother to wear shoes. The impression that I got was that they were either not professional or not too serious about appearing in the selection process. My second doubt was removed when a good number of students applied to appear in the process, leaving or confirming my first impression that the professional attitude was missing. Grooming yourself properly before the interview has several advantages; it helps you make a good impression in the very beginning; it helps you feel confident; it conveys that you are serious about the job that you have applied to. Take care of following:

For Boys

- ✓ Wear a formal shirt and trouser. Usually full sleeves shirts with stripes or simple plain shirts are considered professional. Avoid checkered shirts. Blue, grey and white are safe colours. Don't experiment much with pink, purple, red, black etc. Neck-tie may or may not be worn.
- ✓ Your nails must be clipped properly and should be clean.
- ✓ Get frequent hair-cuts during the interview season. So that if a company is visiting your campus at a short notice, you don't have to run searching for a barber the previous evening. Freshly trimmed hair also looks odd sometimes. Go for a decent hair-style. Too flashy hair-styles often put the interviewer off.
- ✓ Shoes must be formal and should be polished.
- ✓ Another advice for boys. Shave properly before going to the interview. If you keep moustaches, trim them properly.

Also make sure those little whiskers are not peeping out of your nose.

For girls

✓ Wear a decent professional western dress or Kurta-salwaar. Don't wear a saree, if it is not a prescribed uniform for your institute.

✓ Hair must be clean and tidy. Secure them neatly.

✓ Avoid applying make-up. Lipstick and Nail-polish should be very light coloured.

✓ Nails should better be short.

✓ Jewelry should be kept at minimum. Ear rings should be small.

For both Girls and Boys

☒ Don't wear too strong deodorants or perfumes. This habit is usually disliked.

☒ You might be a very firm believer in gemology but believe me numerous rings with colourful stones in your fingers might make a rational interviewer decide not to select you. Your belief in gemology, astrology or other such 'logies' shows that your locus of control is outside you. It shows that your self-esteem is very low. So better remove those rings before going to the interview. One ring is ok.

✓ Wear a watch. It may be a simple watch but it shows that you care about time.

What to carry to interview

What you carry to interview demonstrates your ability to anticipate others' requirements. Carry following things – Two copies of your resume, certificates, a clean note-book, a good pen, your project reports. If informed earlier carry your mark-sheets as well. You may carry all these in a small black or brown colour bag.

Shrugging off nervousness

It is normal to feel butterflies in your stomach just before the interview. Remember what we discussed earlier in chapter – 4, write down your worries for ten minutes before the interview and probably you would have transferred your worries from your head to paper. It will also make you feel more confident. Brain looks at all external stimulus either as a threat or as a reward. Appearing for an interview is classified as a threat and your brain starts preparing your body to fight it out. But, brain doesn't understand the difference between a threat that would require physical preparation and one that requires subtle mental preparation. It increases blood-flow through your body, releases fight or flight hormones and increases your breath rate providing more oxygen to your body. Hyper-oxygenation can make you lightheaded and further increase panic, and a panicky brain is dumber. The best thing about brain is that it responds to thoughts as it responds to reality. Feel yourself talking confidently with the interviewers and tell yourself *"All is well"*. Think about your best moment in life. Tell yourself that you are the best qualified person for this interview. Believe you me, your brain will look forward to the interview and treat it as a reward. Your nervousness will vanish immediately. You may also try to modulate your breathing speed. Consciously bring down your rate of breath. As brain affects the body, your body also affects the brain. If you slow down your breathing, your brain takes it as a signal that everything is all right and that there is no need to fear.

In case the interview cabin is on an upper floor, don't climb stairs if lift is provided. If you have to climb stairs reach there at least 10 minutes before your schedule time. You wouldn't like to be caught panting for air in the interview because of exhaustion. Ensure that even before the interview begins you consciously avoid a nervous body language – clutching one arm with another hand, clutching your thumb in your fist, slouching on the chair, drooping shoulders etc. Psychologists have found that if you fake body-language of a confident person for even as little as 2 minutes, your biology changes and you feel more confident[1].

Ace the Interview

A good beginning is half done. If you have put effort in preparing yourself diligently for the interview, you may walk inside the interview cabin with full confidence. Enter the cabin with a feeling that you have everything that it takes to ace the interview. When you speak with self-confidence others automatically tend to see confidence in you. Remember that the recruiters want to select you. They have committed their entire day to selecting candidates for their requirements. If you radiate confidence it contagiously affects the confidence of the recruiters in you, and with that half of the battle is already won.

As you enter the interview cabin, wear a genuine smile and greet the interviewers. Don't be the first one to offer hand-shake. If they offer then reciprocate with one firm, quick, and warm handshake. Be aware of what time of the day it is and then accordingly say *Good Morning*, *Good After-noon*, or *Good Evening*. Let them indicate where you may sit. Remember that you need to sit with your back straight. Keep your hands in your lap or wherever you feel comfortable. Don't clench your fists, and don't cross your hands in front of your chest. Both these gestures on one hand are signs of nervousness, and on the other they sustain nervousness too. You will notice that once you release tension from your fists and open your arms, a lot of tension will be relieved from your mind too. Don't sit in a rigid posture; but also, don't frequently change your position lest you may appear fidgety. Keep wearing a subtle smile on your face and wait for a response from the interviewers first. Invariably the first question will be *"Tell us something about your-self."* (I am sure you would already have prepared your answer to this question.)

Answer all questions with an authentic voice. Don't sound like you are speaking out a highly practiced answer. Look directly in the eyes of the interviewers while speaking. Provide spaces and pauses at appropriate places in your answer. Don't wait for the interviewer to stop you, stop when you feel that you have answered the question. In case you don't quite understand the question, beg their pardon and ask for the question again.

One common mistake that most candidates do is to jump into answering the question without thinking and structuring the thought process. Some questions require a deliberate and thoughtful answer. While answering such questions you may pause and think a while. Interviewers will actually appreciate that you understand the weight of that particular question and are being thoughtful in answering it. Nevertheless, don't think so deeply that you leave the interviewers wondering when you will finally speak out the words of wisdom.

Try to listen attentively to each question that the interviewer asks. Don't feel that he is there to examine or assess you. For establishing rapport with him, you need to think of him as someone who you like and admire. And, treat the interview as a serious conversation.

Towards the end of the interview, you would generally be given a chance to ask a question. Utilise this part to know something about the profile on offer and the company – What arethe growth plans of the company? What is the career path of a fresh graduate in your company? What are your expectations from a person in this profile?

After the interview seems to be over don't ask if you could take their leave. The interviewers will themselves give you a hint to leave when the interview is over. You can politely thank them with a smile and take your leave.

Interviewers as Human Beings

Interviewers are only human beings and they are bound to oversee psychological traps that may make them take biased and unfair decisions during the interviewing process. Though many companies are aware of this fact and have tried to standardise the recruitment process through practices like Behavioural Event Interviewing (STAR method we read in the previous section), most interviewers still stick to traditional method. Some of the major drawbacks that interviewers suffer from are discussed below.

I still remember attending a behavioural event interview training program. The instructor asked us to do a small role play in which I was required to interview a lady who happened to be a fluent communicator. I was supposed to interview her for Manager-Generalist HR role. I was also provided with the list of characteristics I was supposed to interview her for. An expert in communication skills as she was, the interview lasted with 10 minutes of good chat and discussion about her in general and her career aspirations in specific. At the end of the interview, the instructor asked me for my decision, which obviously for me was 'Yes'. "Here…", the instructor told me," …comes the Halo Effect". The communication skills of this lady and her command over language made me assume that she had got all other qualifications for that job as well. Many interviewers fall victim to "Halo Effect" – where just one of the characteristics of the candidate becomes a proxy for qualification in other criteria for the job also. An exact opposite is "Horn" effect where one shortcoming proves fatal for the candidate. In order to make sure that you don't fall victim to "Horn" effect avoid highlighting a shortcoming, which could be ethically covered up, in the interview. And, needless to say if you have scored highly in your academics or have been an excellent sports person, mention it in the very beginning with stress.

Interviewers also fall prey to "Similarity" trap. Similar backgrounds, educational qualifications, speaking style, dressing style, interests in books or songs, hobbies, etc., tend to make the interviewer assess the candidate favourably. In fact this is one reason that companies grow to have similar people in the organization. It is very difficult to address this issue even with training.

Another unfair but difficult to address trap in interviews is "Stereotypes". Though most of us will deny the existence of any bias or stereotype in our decisions (and with best of our knowledge and intentions), it is difficult to over-ride the implicit biases ingrained in our minds due to social conditioning[2]. Recently an advertisement caught my attention, which is based on an implicit assumption that cricket matches are watched only by men. This is a strong example of Gender Stereotype existing in the advertising industry. You might also observe regional stereotypes: people from North India will always ask for transfer to North, people from certain parts of the country will involve in politics in the organisation, etc. Language and dressing styles might also evoke strong stereotypes and hence affect recruitment decisions. It is difficult for the candidates to affect stereotypical decisions, but there are a few things that you may do to shield yourself from it to some extent. Stereotypes are usually evoked by regional accents, pronunciations, and dressing styles. If you feel that you could be a victim of stereotype during interviews, work on neutralising these factors. Further, you may neutralise regional and language stereotypes by deliberately stating and highlighting that you have lived in different cities and have studied with people from different culture. What you need to understand is that for fighting stereotype you need to prove yourself stronger than it.

Companies often are surprised with an unexpected number of applications when they reach the campuses for recruitment. If they are not prepared to handle so many candidates, they come in a pressure situation where they might, unintentionally, decrease the rigour of the interview process. A decreased rigour implies more dependence on gut-feeling, which is often biased and stereotypical, for making the hiring decision.

Besides these well-known traps affecting recruitment judgments, psychologists have recently identified some very interesting *psychological effects* that might affect our judgment of other people. In 2008, Williams and Bargh conducted an experiment[3] in which they asked a group of people to hold a cup of hot or cold coffee before they were asked to assess the traits of another person. They found that people who held hot coffee before the assessment judged others as warmer and friendlier; while the group with cold coffee did not have a favourable opinion about others. Our brains associate warm temperature with social proximity and friendship, while cold is often coupled with strangers who could be dangerous. These simple associations creep down to affect the way we make our decisions.This has at least two implications for you during the interview:

○ Before you shake hand with the interviewer make sure that your hands are warm and not cold.

○ A cup of coffee or tea in the interviewer's cabin might affect the way they assess you.

Another similar experiment[4] was conducted by *Joshua Ackerman* from the Massachusetts Institute of Technology which showed that the interviewer's assessment about the seriousness and importance of the candidate and his resume increased when the resume was attached to a heavier clip-board in the interviewer's hands. So, the advice: Don't carry your resume/credentials/certificates without any folder or cover. Put it in a nice heavy folder and then provide to the interviewer for his reference. Probably he would attach much more importance to your documents in a folder than without a folder. However, I would like to underscore that the effect studied in the experiment by Ackerman was small but statistically significant. It means it can literally affect the outcome of the interview.

Conclusion

Personal Interview is your chance to highlight your candidature and prove to the interviewer that you have what it takes for getting that job. Preparation for interview begins with a good resume but certainly doesn't stop there. Acing interviews take a lot of concerted effort. Preparing earnestly for both common and company specific questions can help you feel confident during the interview. However, interview is almost always anxiety ridden. Understanding how your brain treats subtle threats like this and puts your body in a hyper-vigilant action ready mode can help you calm down and shrug-off nervousness. Once you have mastered your nervousness you are ready to face the interviewers with an increased level of self-confidence and composure. Interviewers, nevertheless, are also human-beings and have their own fallibilities. Their decisions are often marred by biases, stereotypes and other psychological traps. You need to understand the level of influence that you have on these otherwise uncontrollable factors and take appropriate actions. I would like to end this chapter with one little pep-talk: "In case you are not selected by a particular interview panel, just analyse the reasons and get ready to face the next interview. I have never seen qualified people job-less on street unless they themselves accepted their incompetency. Get ready and give it your best shot! Believe you can make it!"

PART 2
On The Job

Change and Learning

Life is full of changes. In fact it would not be an exaggeration to say that change is the only constant in life. Because change is so ubiquitous, we often adapt gradually and don't even bother about this continuous change. However, it is when the change is discontinuous that we really feel the pain and go through the almost proverbial stages of – Denial, Resistance, Exploration, and Acceptance. Transition from campus to corporate is also fraught with anxieties, apprehensions, and pain because it is discontinuous in more than one sense. In the following chapters we will focus on what are the changes that one encounters in this transition and how one could leverage this change for personal growth.

CHAPTER 6

Transition:
Changes one encounters

The paradox is that although the
knowledge acquired in college is critical
to graduates' success, the process of
succeeding in school is very different
from the process of succeeding at work.
Many of the skills students developed
to be successful in education processes
and the behaviours for which they were
rewarded are not the ones they need to be
successful at work. Worse yet, the culture
of education is so different that when ...
[graduates] continue to have the same
expectations of their employers that they
did of their college professors, they are
greatly disappointed with their jobs and
make costly career mistakes.

— HOLTON (1998)

"Feeling like Alice; tumbling down the rabbit hole?" Morpheus asks *Neo* in the blockbuster sci-fi movie *'Matrix'*. This is the question that I would also ask you here. And, probably, I would get *'yes'* for an answer from you. Only difference being: *You chose to jump down the rabbit hole.* Also, however, I would like to add that this rabbit hole, unlike the one Alice slipped into, would lead you to the world of practicality and business and not one of fantasy. Career, so far for you, was an aspiration, a fantasy, and a dream. This rabbit hole will convert that into reality.

So, what is it that changes so profoundly deserving a complete book on it? Is it that you now got two horns on your head or an extra nose or a few extra limbs? Is it that the world of corporate is a wild place where you need to be cautious lest you fall prey to some scheming colleagues? Is it that the demands put on you would expect you to be a superhuman? Or, would it be a place of continuous stress from unrelenting competition?

I would not build upon these questions, for they are on an extreme which statistics will mark as an exception worthy of ignoring. Change doesn't necessarily mean difficulty and change is not inherently torturous. Rather, it is perceived to be tortuous because it is different. Our brain categorises unfamiliar terrain and uncertainty as a threat to survival. The purpose of this chapter is to reduce that unfamiliarity to some extent by sensitising you to the changes that you might expect to face when you move to corporate from campus. I am supposing with a fair degree of confidence that this realistic preview will certainly help you assuage the anxiety related to the transition and will help in easy assimilation into the world of corporate.

So, what are the changes?

College and Corporate are two distinct entities. They differ in very fundamental ways – in their existential purpose, rules of membership, functioning activities, and bureaucracy. Because of these differences the transition is not a very smooth one. The major changes faced by freshers in an organisation are – *Goals,*

Exhibit 6.1

What does Research Say about Transition from Campus-to-Corporate?

The research landscape is full of findings that highlight the criticality and importance of the transition from college to work. Research has established that less than 50% of the college graduates stay with their first company after 2 years. The average tenure is 11 years. These findings highlight that there is something amiss in either the way new-comers are handled by the organizations or the way the students are prepared to handle the transition. Several of the studies have established the direct relationship between newcomer adjustment and early exit. Some of the reasons for adjustment related problems as identified by research are: Change in culture, lack of experience and skills required by the employer, unrealistic expectations from work-life, Lack of structure at work and Role reversal – from a college senior to junior employee.

Reference: Addressing the College-to-Work Transition – Nancy M. Wendlandt and Aaron B. Rochlen

PS: These are international studies; but human psychology is essentially the same. If the findings are true for other countries they must be so for Indian students, at least to some degree.

what you work towards; *Accountability*, who are you answerable to; *Managing Yourself,* the way you manage your time, manage your emotions, motivate yourself, manage your stress; *Review and Assessment,* how is your performance judged and assessed; *Learning,* how you improve yourself; *Relationships,* who you work with and get work done through; *Culture,* what are the guiding values, beliefs, and assumptions of people around you.

In following pages we will deal with each of these changes in detail and would discuss how these changes make a difference to the way you work.

Goals: Getting a job to doing a job

Psychologists have purported several theories of motivation. The underlying denominator of most of these motivation theories is "Need". One of the earliest and most successful and appealing theories is "Maslow's need hierarchy". According to this theory humans have needs at five levels. Need at a lower level has to be satisfied before a person feels the need at a higher level. The five levels are; *Physiological,* basic needs related to food and nutrition; *Safety,* needs related to shelter and protection; *Social,* need to relate with others; *Self Esteem,* need to be respected; *Self Actualisation,* need to realise one's actual potential. According to this theory the goals that a person has keep changing when the need at a particular level is fulfilled or achieved. For example, a person who is not able to fulfill the basic requirements of life like food, clothes and shelter, will not feel the need for respect from others. His lower level needs will be more overwhelming and demanding.

It is *"needs"* that determine *"goals"*. As you move from campus to corporate the *"need"* changes from getting a break to rising up in the career. So the *goal* also changes in context. All along in your college life one thing that bothered you most was whether you would get a decent job after you finished your course (Obviously, students coming from well-off families might not have such a burning desire to get a job, possibly because their needs at lower levels are already fulfilled.) The *goal* in student life: *Get a job.* Getting good marks, earning certificates, attending training program, and extra-curricular activities are often just means to this end. But, when you join your new job you should expect to have new goals related to learning and performance. However, things are not that clear here – ambiguities abound.

When you get the job, after initial moments of joy, you would be surprised to see that you don't know what to do next. While in the college things were highly structured, here it might be thoroughly unstructured. When you join your job, first few weeks might be quite confusing as you won't know what you are supposed to achieve further. Many young trainees are bewildered by the fact that they are not given any concrete goals in the first few months of their job and are often asked to run errands. This approach by the organisations is not justified; nevertheless, if you are caught up in such a situation it is better to understand that the organisation is just providing you time to understand the system informally and learn through your own efforts at work. It is only when you learn through this "sink or swim" technique and win trust of your senior colleagues (read boss) by doing small, seemingly menial, jobs that you are ready for more responsible tasks and activities.

In case you are lucky, your new organisation might provide you with a list of small learning goals that you are supposed to finish during your training period. This structured approach is not followed by many organisations. However, I would like to mention that a structured approach to learning is often more effective than the less considerate – "*Throw them in the ocean, and they will learn to swim*". No doubts, learning happens through experience but then in how much time and at what cost?!

Anyway, the aim of this section is not to criticise and compare different methodologies that organisations follow, but to make you aware that these methodologies exist and if you were to find yourself in one of those you would know that you are not being particularly marked out. The test of prince is that he has to prove himself in the worst circumstances – the heir to the throne could not expect authority to be given in a platter.

So, when you move to job you might have either no defined goal or concrete well-defined goals. Let's deal with them one-by-one. The former case is a classic case and new recruits behave in a variety of manner in this situation. Most people, in such a case, decide to spend time in cafeteria with other like-minded new recruits; many feign that they are busy sitting long hours behind computer screens; some actually approach HR and whine about their situation; few decide to take it up with their bosses and chart out learning and performance goals for themselves. The best way out in this case is actually the last one but only a few choose it.

The latter case is found in a few organisations having vintage trainee schemes. In this case you might find that goals are impersonal and might even appear to be redundant rigmarole. While goals in the college time were related only to you, everyone in the organisation (College) helped you achieve it, in corporate you will find that goals are related to the organisation and other people in the organisation are working towards their own goals (Though, the goals are ultimately related). If you don't have a passion to learn and perform, you might not feel motivated enough to achieve these goals. You have to see beyond the obvious and understand the wider business perspective to achieve those goals. Needless to say, without interpersonal effectiveness most of the goals will be almost impossible to achieve, unlike in college where you could top the college without even speaking to your teachers.

Managing Yourself

After working for close to 10 years now, I sometimes remember the time I was in college. Managing time was not a difficult task with a few simple demands from life. I am not sure if everybody would agree with me on this, but at least people who have led a simple enough life would do.

Entry into work-life turned my perspective about the simplicity of life on its head. While goals become unstructured suddenly, the flexibility of arranging one's schedule goes off equally suddenly because of unrelenting demands: demands from bosses (some people are unfortunate enough to have more than one boss), demands from colleagues, demands from your own career aspirations, demands from personal life, demands & more demands, relentlessly pulling you in different directions.

To worsen the matter further, it is difficult to judge which demand has higher priority and which one is just another distraction. *What is urgent? What is Important? What to do immediately? What to put on hold? What to drop once for all?* These are the questions that your work will ask you to answer perpetually.

Like this was not enough, you also have to make such difficult decisions: *Who to approach? Who to avoid? Who to appease? Who to be careful about? Who is politically strong? Who can be your ally? Who will stall your plans? Who needs to support your plans?* And so on…And, there would be no readily available right answers.

Emotions also run high on certain days and you have to be careful about the way you behave: How to handle your frustrations? How to help when your panic buttons are pressed? How to manage resulting stress? How to manage cool when things are not going as per the plan?

This is the time that you will desperately seek help on obscure topics like Time Management, Stress Management, Emotional Intelligence, Personal Effectiveness and things like that. We will discuss all this in detail later in the book.

Accountability: Who do you work for?

Ever fancied what would happen if, god forbid, you flunked your exams? Who will be affected? Who will care? Probably, your parents will be sad, your teachers disappointed, and your friends sympathetic. But, in the long run it is you who is going to be affected. An entire year of your life will be wasted. The gaps in your study will gape at you from your resume throughout your life. You will find yourself explaining it to recruiters. So, while you study, you are the only person you are truly working for and are accountable to.

Now, behold, you are working in a company, say as a sales manager. Imagine yourself able to achieve only 50% of the sales target. You get a "Below Expectations" in your performance appraisal. No raise. No promotion (Must be feeling quite sick by now). But besides you, it is the company which lost revenue. It is the stakeholders whose probable dividends got reduced. Take it further, imagine yourself getting irritated with a customer and shouting obscenities at him. What happens next, who is affected? You? Yes. But, do you think that the company has any chances of retaining this customer? Not remotely! Each and every action of you affects, besides you, your company and other people associated with it.

In campus-to-corporate training program, I try to emphasise this big difference. **You pay to get educated but you are paid to work.** This difference is because of extended accountability that you take on when you move into work life. You are accountable to parties who entrust you with a responsibility and compensate you for that in monetary or non-monetary form. This accountability demands from you that you demonstrate thoughtful and responsible behaviour at work place. Your actions should be in line with the general expectations of the company and the organisation.

However, responsibility is earned in most organisations. The first few years of your job are supposed to be a learning phase. As the company pays you, the management expects you to pick the tricks and skills of the trade. You are accountable and answerable to them for learning, in addition you might also be assigned some low risk responsibilities. Based on your performance your responsibility level is increased gradually. People who ask for more responsibility before proving themselves worthy of it or who raise issues about compensation even before delivering performance are often disliked in organisations.

Review and Assessment

The primary mean of assessing your performance in colleges is written examination. The objective of written examination is to measure how much have you learned in terms of concepts, facts, and other objective and established knowledge. Come to corporate world and here you are assessed through the process called 'Performance Appraisal'. Performance Appraisal is supposed to be an extended discussion between a superior and his/her subordinates on their performance. The objective of performance appraisal is to find-out, through a dialogue process, level of achievements of your goals, your learning and training needs, future directions, etc.

If written examination is on the extreme end of objectivity, performance appraisals have been (and are still in most organisations) on the extreme end of subjectivity. The outcome of performance appraisals doesn't depend entirely on your performance at work, your performance at the dialogue, or even your competencies (Nevertheless, these factors really affect it a lot.) It also depends to a large extent on what your superior thinks of you, what your colleagues think of you, and what is the culture in the organisation. Handling performance appraisals is often a challenge for both the appraiser and the appraisee. The organisations are conscious to this fact and that is why more and more organisations are taking active steps in ensuring that their performance management systems are fool-proof, transparent and as objective as possible.

Besides performance appraisals, you will also find that companies do have a review system that goes on continually throughout the year at different levels. At department levels, you will have morning meetings, weekly meetings and monthly meetings; at project level you will have regular project review meetings; at business level, you will have monthly and quarterly meetings. The purpose of all these meetings is also to check if things are going on as per plan. While performance appraisals were supposed to be for assessment at individual level, these meetings provide a mechanism to keep a tab on the performance of teams and other groups of people.

So, when you come to the corporate, the review and assessment system is more spread-out, more subjective, but more rigorous.

The Way You Learn

In junior school we had almost no control over the subjects that we were taught. Someone, somewhere had already decided what we were supposed to learn. In High-school we had more freedom to choose our area of study. But, it was not till college level that we decided completely the stream which we wanted to specialise in. However, even in college we hardly had any say on the methodology that the institute adopted to teach us. The learning was still directed and driven from outside us. This way of learning is based on the premise that the teacher knows what the student is supposed to learn and that it is possible to transfer learning in the classroom from the teacher to the student. This methodology works, no doubts, but it leaves us poorly equipped with tools for self-directed, self-driven learning which is required once you are in a job. No! I am not saying that we can't keep learning the similar way throughout our lives. We can certainly keep reading books and keep attending training programs, conferences, seminars to learn this way. Rather, I am saying that we are poorly equipped to learn that which we don't know we need to learn. We don't learn how to solve problems, how to manage self, how to manage others, how to be creative and innovative, how to work in teams, how to mentor others, how to .... ; the list is endless. You might find a lot of self-help books, management books, how-to books on these topics, but believe me, all these 'how-to's are better learnt following another methodology: Experiential Learning. We have come across this term earlier in the book and I am reserving an entire chapter to discuss just this. So wait till the next chapter where we will discuss what exactly is experiential learning and how you may catalyse it.

Relationships: New Definitions

(Wo) man is a social animal. It is not possible for us to live all by ourselves. There are only a few things that we can achieve working alone. Organisations we work in have goals that are impossible without collective efforts. As you enter the organisation you would realise that most of your work depends besides you on a number of other people around you. The most significant among them are your Boss and your colleagues. So far, you had lived a life in which these new relationships didn't exist. You had parents, siblings, friends, relatives, and teachers. You had these relationships since you were a kid and you knew pretty well how to deal with these relationships. However, these new relationships are nothing like the old ones. These relationships exist to get something done. There is no emotional basis for their existence. But since you are not conditioned for these relationships you might start confusing them with some of the relationships you already know about. Boss is treated like a parent or a teacher, colleagues are treated like friends and people who you don't interact much become strangers.

This confusion is the root of many interpersonal problems that new people often encounter at work. This is a big change that newcomers to the organisations need to be sensitised to. At work, relationships are professional, not personal. You should not attach a dry, unemotional connotation to the word "professional" because this word denotes the purpose behind the relationship. This purpose is very important and 'sacred' in some sense. We need to give it the recognition and respect that it deserves.

We will discuss in detail on this topic later in the book.

Culture

Whenever you see a group of people you will realise that they have a typical way of working and behaving. They will have a particular vocabulary, temperament, likes, dislikes, beliefs, mores (mo-RAYs), rites and rituals. This is what you call culture of those people.As this is true of nations, this is equally true of organisations as well.

In an organisation people come together to achieve something beyond the capability of an individual. In achieving this something they have to take decisions pertaining to tasks, delegation of authority, distribution of work, distribution of rewards, defining processes, establishing procedures, recruiting new people, and rites and rituals. These decisions are taken based on certain assumptions, values, and beliefs which form as the organisation grows while dealing with external and internal challenges.

This culture might be quite a change to deal with for new entrants and it takes time to understand and adapt to it before they could start performing. We have a chapter waiting towards the end to give you an insight into how organisations work.

Conclusion

Work life is very different from college life. This difference is the main reason for the diffi culties that new recruits face when they join their first job. The main differences are in the types of goals, assessment of performance, types of relationships, the way of learning and the culture of the organisation. Being aware of these changes can let you have realistic expectations from your work life and would assuage the pain that might result from the abrupt, discontinuous change that you encounter when you join your first job.

CHAPTER 7

Experiential Learning:
A whole new way of learning

Book's Intention

Mulla Naseerudeen asked his 10 year old son to climb up the tree. When he had climbed some 10 feet, he asked him to jump. The son refused. It was too high for him to jump. He was afraid he might hurt himself. Mulla insisted. He assured that he would catch him as he jumped and that he didn't need to worry. Son obeyed his father's command and jumped hoping he would be saved. As soon as he jumped he realised that his father quickly jumped to one side as he fell down on the fl oor with a thud His knees hit the ground and pained badly. Mulla came over him and said, "Never trust anybody, not even your father."

Experience has always been considered a great teacher. Mulla Naseerudeen used it to teach his son the pessimistic, untrustworthy side of human nature. But Mulla made an assumption in his teaching methodology. He thought that his son after experiencing the deceitful behaviour of his own father and a reflective lesson after it would take this learning by heart. But this is not what happens in real life. You have an experience; you reflect and ponder over it to formulate new concepts. These concepts are again put into practice and give rise to new experiences, which are further reflected upon to provide refined concepts ready to be tested again. This cycle keeps on going. We had discussed this learning cycle in chapter-2. Mulla's son probably would have grown up with this non-trusting attitude but soon he would have realised through his experiences that there were people who were trustworthy and that his simple rule-of-thumb about people was indeed very limited in approach.

It is no news that with experience you gain insights that improve your knowledge about how the world works. And that is the precise reason that organisations put you higher up in the hierarchy and are ready to pay you more if you have more years of experience in your resume. But does experience teach equally well to everyone; I don't agree. If this were so, people with same number of years of experience would be equally intelligent or wise, and we know this is not the case.

It is all too easy to live life rushing from one task to another – getting up in the morning and going to office, finishing tasks one after another, coming back, watching TV, reading a book, talking with spouse, playing with children. Stopping to think and reflect is a luxury that one has to improvise and make provision for. Experiential learning cycle, like a bicycle or motor-cycle, needs a prime-mover, which in this case is conscious effort to learn by creating situations that push one to learn. If we don't convert our experiences into learning through reflection, abstract conceptualisation, and experimentation, we are running the least risk of repeating the same mistakes again and again and a major risk of not being able to respond to gradual change that is an integral part of our lives. In this chapter you will learn how learning takes place at work-place and how you can leverage this knowledge to push yourself unflinchingly towards improving yourself and your performance.

Crucibles – Finding Experiences to Learn From

Warran Bennis, in an article[1] published in HBR *"Crucibles of Leadership"*, used the term *crucible* for experiences that help a person grow as a leader. In medieval times Alchemists tried to convert base metals, by mixing and heating them, into gold in small vessels called crucibles. A crucible is hot (metaphor for discomfort); it upgrades the metal inside it. So crucible is a metaphor for experiences which are uncomfortable and which help a person grow internally. For experiential learning you need to find such crucibles for yourself – crucibles where you leave the safety and security of home turf behind.

There are two time tested ways that can provide you these crucibles:

Change in territory[2]

As long as you stay in a territory that you are familiar with it is difficult, if not impossible, to grow. Territory could be geographical, but it could be technical or functional as well. When you work in a familiar terrain, you are comfortable and with comfort, come a false sense of security. I am sure you would have heard the story of the boiling frog. If you put a frog in boiling water, it will immediately jump off. However, if you keep it in cold water and heat it slowly, the frog gets cozy and comfortable. It doesn't realise when the water starts boiling and it eventually dies in the boiling water. The slow change doesn't let the frog brace up to act on it. This is what happens when you get more and more comfortable in a particular territory. As everything is familiar you don't notice the small changes and don't learn to adapt to those changes and when you realise it, your fate is already decided.

Exposing yourself deliberately to a change lets you realise your shortcomings and thus force you to work on improving upon them. Change in territory is a powerful prime-mover. It provides a fertile ground for learning and self-improvement.

There are plenty of ways in which you can try to put yourself in this crucible.

- Does your company work in more than one geographical location? Try to find out if you could be given a project at a location which you are not familiar with. Moving to a new location provides you the opportunity to work with people who are different from you; different in language, culture, beliefs, ways of working and perspectives. These differences are many times so stark that they make you question some of your own beliefs, ways of working and perspectives, which you would have taken for granted. This questioning is nothing but the second stage of the experiential learning cycle: Reflective Observation. Through it you end up with new concepts ready to be experimented again.

- Is there a challenge in your organisation that is bothering more than one function (department)? Try to collaborate with members from other teams and launch a cross-functional team for addressing this challenge. When you work on challenges that go beyond a certain function, you get an outside in perspective through the eyes of those who see your team from outside. It again helps you change and refine your concepts about how things work.

- If your company has a policy for Job-rotation, request your boss to expose you to different parts of your function. After a few years of experience, even change in function is recommended for further growth. Vertical growth (across hierarchy) is more achievable and sustainable when it is built on a solid horizontal growth spanning different functional responsibilities and achievements.

- Embrace change. Change is the factor that helps you evolve.

Crises

Before I start elaborating this point, I would like to state unequivocally that don't create crises by procrastination. If you are able to manage your time and work well, chances are that you would avoid converting the simple situations into crises. However, the world is an unpredictable place. Crises are bound to come, if not of your own doing then someone else's. Crisis brings the best out of people. It pushes them beyond their self-defined and inhibiting boundaries. And, human potential once stretched never regains its earlier dimensions.

Crises have this uncanny ability to bring the best out of people because of some typical characteristics[3]

- Crises make it a question of now or never. There is no question of procrastination. It is urgent. It is in your face. It is very costly to not respond to a crisis.
- In crises people help each other. They empathise and support each other.
- In crises you don't look at constraints but look at innovative ways of overcoming them. Rules are rewritten during crises.
- In crises you do whatever it takes to succeed. You discover new strengths. You end up more confident of yourself.

Finally,

- In crises results are to be seen almost immediately.

As said earlier, you shouldn't create crises by procrastination. But, you can't also wait for crises to develop before you learn from them. If you could, however, create situations at your work that have characteristics that we discussed above, you might mimic a crisis and gain associated benefit of learning. Some of the ways you might achieve it are

- Divide your deliverables in smaller chunks and treat each chunk as a deliverable in itself. Commit a deadline for these chunks to your boss or whoever is the stakeholder.

- Have an arrangement with a colleague to review your progress on important but not urgent deliverables.
- Take up assignments that challenge your current level of skills.
- Join others when they are fighting with a crisis of their own. Offer help. Treat it as your own.
- Celebrate small successes.

Besides these, whenever a real crisis comes, face it with a confidence that you will overcome it. Take it as an opportunity to better yourself.

This is not Learning

There are so many things that may be mistaken for learning. Many people spend their lives hoarding knowledge from books, magazines and so many other sources. That is not learning. Many others try to gain knowledge by going through formal training or study. That also is not learning. Still others go through experiences thinking learning will happen automatically. Now, that certainly is not learning. Learning is much more than all these things. It happens when a person consciously desires and endeavours to become better at what he does. It also happens when he goes out finding solutions to the problems he sees around himself. And, he could be certain that he has learnt something, when he finds that he has developed a new better habit, adopted a better view or model of the world, and has used it to grow not only himself but others around him. Now, that is what we call *learning*.

Exhibit 7.1

Reflection: Transforming Experience into Concepts

An unexamined life is not worth living - Socrates

One of my ex-Bosses used to call us after every major activity that the team did. It used to be an exercise in which we used to try to answer following questions

- What did we do?
- How did it go?
- How do we feel about it?
- How could it be done even better?
- What do we do now?

The results of these meetings used to be very insightful and helped us improve our performance almost continuously. This is exactly what reflection implies. It means thinking about the experience that you have gone through to cull out learning and action plans for future. Experiences can be addictive. People who like immersing themselves in experiences often go from one experience to another never halting to ponder over them. This approach leads to a gut-based, implicit learning, which is often immune to refinement and change. Charles Handy, one of the most influential management thinkers, in his book *"Understanding Organizations"* tells about a successful businessman who had earned millions of pounds at a relatively young age. Charles Handy met him at a Management Institute attending a management development program. Quite surprised, Charles Handy asked him, "Why are you coming here as a student? With your record you should join the faculty?". "I have come to find out why I am so successful?" the young man replied. This man clearly understood that it was necessary to stop and reflect at his experience to derive learning and ensure sustenance of the success he had achieved. In order to push the cycle of learning further a conscious approach to reflection is required. You need to stop from time-to-time and reflect over what happened and transform your experience into articulated learning.

How do you do it?

Journaling

Writing Journal or Diary is a very effective and powerful way of reflection. Psychologists have highlighted several therapeutic benefits of journaling. People who write about their experiences are healthier both physically and mentally than those who don't. Besides the therapeutic uses Journaling is a powerful way for increasing self-awareness, finding meaning in life-experiences, planning further, and focusing one's thoughts[4]. As you write down your experiences, you are forced to analyse, evaluate, and judge them from a third person perspective. It helps you appraise the experience and your performance in it from an objective perspective. You often question your own assumptions and beliefs while observing your own behaviour while writing. This leads to new insights and learnings. Writing even for as short as 10 minutes or so is also beneficial. The best format that I ever encountered for this reflective exercise was in study material from the workshop on Technology of Participation by Institute of Cultural Affairs. It had four steps:

Step 1 – Write down objectively what happened

Step 2 – Write down how it impacted you, emotionally or otherwise

Step 3 – Write down what implications and learning do you drive from the event

Step 4 – Write down how the entire event, impact and implications integrate with your life

Dialogues

Focused dialogues with colleagues or friends on your experiences also help you transform your experiences into learning. Dialogues let you on one hand revisit the experience and reappraise it in hindsight and on the other lets you view it from another person's perspective as well. Dialogue is an effective tool for reflection but you have to be careful with certain things:

- You should go with an intention to learn from the experience
- You should be ready to listen even to not-so-self-assuring comments also. Don't defend yourself. Accept the comments as they come.
- You need to trust the person you are talking to.

- Person you are talking to should be interested in your development.
- Don't let the dialogue stray away in any other direction or to some other topic.

Visualising

This is the simplest method for reflection if you could master the difficult art of visualisation. You just need to find 10 minutes and think about your day. Visualise yourself going through your day. What is that you did? Who did you meet? What challenges came? How did you face them? After visualisation think about what could you have done differently. Make notes after visualisation exercise if possible.

Observing others

So far we have discussed how you could learn from your own experiences. It is not required to go through experiences in order to learn from the art of reflection. You may even learn by watching and observing the behaviours of those around you as well. Identify a person who is considered effective and successful in your organisation. Watch him keenly in action whenever you get opportunity. Note the behaviours he demonstrates which differentiate him from others and practice them. Movies and biographies are also source of learning through reflective observation.

Abstract Concepts, Hypotheses and Working Models

In school and college we are taught concepts to work with. These concepts are very well defined. They come complete with definitions, relationships between various components, models, and areas of applications. It is because these concepts are so detailed that we can apply them as such or with slight improvisation in solving problems.

When you start working you realise that challenges you face can be clubbed into types or categories: people management challenges, time management challenges, self-management challenges and so on. These categories are further divided into sub-categories. As you deal with these challenges you realise that you start building some tacit rules of behaviour or heuristics for decision making. These tacit rules and heuristics are nothing but your abstract concepts about handling the challenges at hand. We have seen earlier, whatever is tacit is difficult to refine. Something that is vague can't be improved. That is why it is necessary to be aware of your abstract concepts. The articulated concepts and models help us solve practical problems with relative ease. Concepts and models are rarely perfect. They are usually approximate and have to be taken with a pinch of salt. But, you can always try to improve an existing model.

There are several sources of concepts and models:

Books, are a rich source of knowledge. You can learn a lot from them. Keep a note-book where you jot down in a simpler way some of the important learnings from each book that you read. Try to read at least 1 book a month. Keep your reading eclectic.

Others' Experiences can provide you a lot of concepts and models of how things work. Many people are especially good at explaining their beliefs about things elaborately in form of diagrams and equations. You can identify opportunities and gain knowledge from such people. However, you need to put to test those beliefs before you accept them.

As you put yourself in different crucibles as discussed earlier and reflect on them by writing journals or engaging in learning dialogues, **your own experiences** get transformed into abstract concepts and models. You need to consciously put them to tests to see their reliability and validity to further refine them.

Attending **workshops & training programs** is also a simple and effective way of gaining access to a variety of time tested concepts and models. Identify which areas you want to work on and attend training program and workshops in your organisation or even outside to continue improving your knowledge base.

Internet has now become an answer to almost every type of query that a person might have. It obviously has a vast database of knowledge. However, I have found that Internet could be quite confusing as there are contradictory views on each topic. It is very difficult to decide what is right and what is wrong. But notwithstanding the ambiguous nature of the information on internet as a whole, there still are websites which are relatively more credible than others. Look for websites of big consultancy organisations, universities, renowned authors, and academicians. They can be a relevant source of knowledge that you might use. Blogs can be misleading sometimes but they can still provide you some food for thought.

Hypothesis Testing: Experimentation

Learning takes place only when we are open to test our assumptions, beliefs, hypotheses, mental models, and current knowledge. In case we throw these things beyond a veil of false intellectual arrogance and pride, it becomes difficult to continue learning. Defensive reasoning and mindset deter learning and personal growth. Even for subjective topics we have to adopt the mindset of a curious scientist, who builds a hypothesis and then tests it. He will keep rejecting and bettering his hypothesis till it is confirmed through his experiments. Yet he is aware that the scientific community will not think twice before rejecting an established concept or theory if there is just one exception to it.

Experimentation is the final and the most important part of learning. It helps you establish the true learning. It lets you keep evolving. It gives you confidence that you are moving in the right direction.

As an active experimenter in an organisation, whenever you put forward proposals, design something new, adopt a new behaviour, take an initiative, follow these advices:

- – Be conscious of the assumptions, models, beliefs, and concepts behind your actions.
- – Monitor and record results.
- – Take feedback.
- – Compare with other proposals/designs/behaviours/ initiatives
- – Make changes if required
- – Continue experimenting.

Conclusion

Learning in classroom and learning in an organisation are different. Once you start working you need to learn continuously from experience. Experiential learning has four stages – Concrete Experience, Reflective Observation, Abstract Conceptualisation, and Active Experimentation (*David Kolb*). It may be stymied without conscious effort from your side. You need to actively find ways of putting yourself in experiences that provide you food for reflection; reflect using different techniques like, journaling, dialogues, etc; develop abstract concepts through reflection, experience sharing and reading; and, finally do hypothesis testing through experimentation.

Understanding and Managing Self

As soon as you get in your work place your mind will be overwhelmed with organisational dynamics, processes, procedures, planning, goals, politics and other related things. It is very simple here to get so involved with things outside you that you forget looking back at yourself. You forget that you are in driver's seat and that you have a claim and access to your rational decision making process. As your brain processes the plethora of information and data coming from outside it switches on to an auto-mode which might not be yet adapted to deal with the situations. The results: Anxiety, Sour Relationships, Unfinished Goals, No Self-Development. It is a time where you need to stop and look in the mirror, to manage your anxieties, to take rational emotionally intelligent decisions, to work on your weaknesses and to leverage your strengths.

CHAPTER 8

Anxiety: Managing it-Leveraging it

"Then you are only a mocking demon,
and I mistook you for someone of power"

**"Buddha – A Story of Enlightenment",
by Deepak Chopra**

Evolution has been a heartless and merciless creator. It made organisms as mere *"survival machines"*. To survive in the chaotic world of millions of years back, our ancestors had to quickly react to the stimuli existing in their environment. They had to quickly judge if the situation around them was one in which they could relax or one in which they should be circumspect and fight or flee: Was the environment friendly or hostile? The effectiveness of this judgment meant they survived and helped them pass on those genes to their offspring which bestowed this capability to gauge the danger in the environment. It was better to overestimate the danger and react to it by fighting or fleeing 100% of times than to take risk and die 60% of times (or anything other than 100%). Being overcautious paid in those days. The design of our brain thus was guided by one principle: *Better Safe Than Dead*. We are the offspring of those overcautious beings and have retained the same instinct to perceive the situation as more dangerous than it really is. And, that instinct today results in worry and anxiety whenever we have the slightest of a hint of being in danger, however subtle.

Anxiety and Stress: Necessary Evil

Anxiety – coming out of our suspicion about our environment – was required to survive in the much hostile days that our ancestors spent in the jungle. It is still required today, for it coupled with the stress it produces, in short term, improves focus, memory and creativity. Anxiety in some amount is required and is indispensable for performance. It is when anxiety and stress remain for prolonged periods that they become toxic. The stress hormones released when we expect danger prepare us for fighting it in short-term at the expense of long term physical and mental growth. However, anxiety beyond certain level could be paralysing even in short-term.

More than a century ago two Harvard Professors, Robert M Yerkes and John D Dodson calibrated the relationship between anxiety (or stress) and performance. They found that the performance of people increases with increase in anxiety for some time before peaking and then declines with further increase in anxiety.

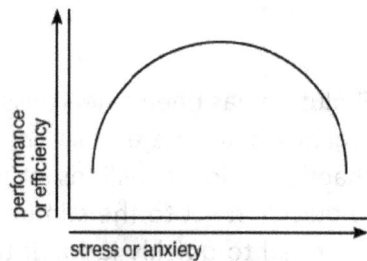

Figure 8.1

The level of stress or anxiety that brings out the best in people is different for different people and may even increase as a person gains more experience and skills in his work.

Besides performance, learning itself is driven by anxiety. According to a leading Organisation Psychologist – Edgar Schein – Learning is associated with two types of anxieties: Learning Anxiety, related to apprehensions about capability, social implications, self-esteem; and, Survival Anxiety, related to implications of not being able to learn. Learning happens when Survival Anxiety is more than Learning Anxiety.

So, anxiety and stress are a part of learning and performance with which the organisations are mostly concerned. It is no surprise then that Organisations are a source of lot of stress and anxieties. It is only up to us to harness it to our benefit and not let it debilitate our performance and success in our careers.

Organisations: Source of Unending Anxieties and Stress

Organisations are a source of lot of worries that stem from different sources. A newcomer to an organisation can be overwhelmed by these worries which may drastically reduce the learning and performance – thanks to the limited capacity of our brains – and may even cause chronic stress.Since anxieties are often due to things that are more a figment of your imagination than reality, to be successful it thus becomes very important that you know when this anxiety is warranted and when not; you wouldn't like to waste your bandwidth worrying about baseless apprehensions.In this chapter, we will discuss how to discern a genuine source of anxiety from an imaginary and baseless worry; how to handle common genuine sources of anxiety and stress; and how to reduce the harmful impacts and get the most out of a seemingly difficult and anxiety ridden situation.

Uncertainty about your role

When I joined my first job, I realised that I was sent to my department by the Corporate Office and the head of the department had not asked for that position (I didn't know at that time that Management Trainees are often recruited for being groomed for future and not for immediate requirements.). I was asked to work along with other colleagues and learn. The questions that haunted me for several following months were – What was my role, my position? What was I supposed to learn? How was I supposed to learn? The uncertainties about my position were too overwhelming and at that time I didn't know how to handle them. The uncertainties vanished the moment, my boss came out with a goal sheet for me with well-defined control points (metrics). But, by that time, I had already wasted several precious months.

Exhibit 8.1

Role Ambiguity

When you and your boss differ in your opinions of your role, role ambiguity comes. Role ambiguity might be further exacerbated by differing expectations from peers and customers. Whatever organisations do to define the role through job descriptions and goal setting exercises, role ambiguity problem is to remain because of volatile situations prevailing in most of the organisations. Norman Maier and two colleagues in 1958 reported that when they asked senior managers in several companies to define role of the subordinate they knew best, only 35% of the times did they match with the role definitions by the subordinates themselves. Though the study is old, I doubt if the results would be any different if such a study is carried out today.

In many organisations newcomers are often left to themselves for learning. They are not told or guided about what they are supposed to do? How their work will be evaluated? How they will advance in their career? And, what is the scope of their responsibility? In such an uncertain situation the newcomers often find themselves worrying about their Roles and Responsibilities. In case there is lack of resources and feedback, the situation worsens further. Even in organisations where well-established training processes for fresh graduates exist, an uncertainty about expectations may arise. You have to brace yourself for facing such uncertainties and handling your anxiety. Take this anxiety as a signal that you are not fully occupied with work. Let it push you towards identifying areas where you may learn and make a contribution. Anxieties when treated as a signal rather than a symptom can actually help you get the best out of you. There are certain things that you may do for handling such situations:

- Approach your boss and request him to assign you a few projects or goals. In most cases your boss will be happy with your proactive approach and help you devise a plan for a few months. Bosses are also human beings and are not perfect as you might like them to be. Moreover, they are not mind-readers. You need to share your feeling with them and ask for support.

- Make a Discovery Notebook – a notebook where you write questions and then set out to find answers to those questions. You may write questions in following categories: Company, about its history, values, business, challenges, opportunities, competitions etc; Processes, how things get done;People, what is the demography in the organisation. You may write questions in other categories as well. As you go around getting answers to these questions – you will meet new people and learn a lot of new things.

- Find out what organisation improvement initiatives are being taken. Volunteer for playing a role in such initiatives.

- Identify what training programs your organisation conducts. Attend the few which are relevant to you.

Always remember that when role is ambiguous, look at the goal. If goal is clear, role doesn't matter.

Boss: The Hari Sadu

Sam had always been like that. His managing principle was – "Most people don't work unless they are forced and pushed continuously". He had a Photo Frame put up in his cabin. A placard below it read "Loser of the Month". Whenever he was unhappy with someone he used to put his photograph there for everybody to see.

According to Gallup International when people leave their jobs they leave their bosses rather than the organisations[1]. An article published in McKinsey Quarterly[2] reported that for more than 75% percent of people, dealing with the boss is the most stressful aspect of their work. The article further said that Bosses could literally kill you. It quoted a Swedish study of 3122 men for 10 years that showed that people with bad bosses suffer heart attack 20-40% times more than normal people.

Nevertheless, bosses are not to be blamed. It is people who promote them to be bosses without training them properly who are responsible for messing up. Most people who are bosses today started their careers as individual contributors. They were technical or functional people who must have been good at their work. However, being good at one's work doesn't necessarily make one a good Manager. Being a Manager is a difficult task at which most people fail utterly. They result in demotivated workforce and sub-optimal performances. If you find yourself working under such a boss it might be quite traumatic. Bad bosses come in different types – over demanding, micro-managing, over-delegating, incompetent, outrightly rude – but they have the same impact: All bad bosses result in demotivated, stressed and sapped out employees who underperform and leave the organisation whenever an opportunity throws up.

If you are unfortunate enough to feel that you have got a boss who fits any of the criteria discussed above, you need to worry about your worries. The amount of anxiety and stress you are risking is worthy of one more worry – about your psychological and physiological health. If you realise that you have got a bad boss you need to take charge and save yourself from possible devastating impact.

– First thing that you need to do is accept your situation. Tell yourself that this is an opportunity to learn how to handle difficult people. Decide to get best out of this situation for yourself – after all God didn't send you to earth with a guarantee that everything will flow smoothly. When you are in front of a Tiger, you can't curse your bad luck, you need to run, or do whatsoever, to save your life. Focus on action not on cause of problem.

– Before jumping to the conclusion that your boss is bad, provide him benefit of doubt. Check if it is your own bias, fear, incompetence that is colouring your perception. Check if your judgement is really correct and free of subjectivity. Talk to others who have worked with him for longer duration (without divulging your opinion). You may ask them some simple open-ended questions about the team and not directly about the boss. It would help you shroud the questions and it wouldn't look like you are trying to confirm your judgment of your boss.

  ○ What have been the main achievements of the department?

  ○ How are the team decisions taken?

  ○ How do performance reviews happen?

  ○ What are the development areas of the Team?

While you listen to the answers pay attention to what they have to say about the role, contribution or behaviour of your boss. You might get to know a lot from these conversations. You might actually end up nullifying your assumptions about your boss and might give him a more empathetic consideration thereon.

– Try to talk to your boss and ask for feedback from time-to-time. You might be provided with a shattering and heartbreaking feedback but that will ensure that you know which of your shortcomings or behaviours might be troubling him. Thank him for the feedback that he provides.

– Understand your Boss's priorities. Ask for his support in fixing your goals and performance standards. Once established keep informing him about the status even when not asked for. Bad Boss or Good Boss, you need to partner with him.

– If your Boss micromanages, don't worry. Being a fresher it is actually good for you.

– If your boss is incompetent, find a mentor elsewhere in the organisation.

– If your boss has an abdicative style, trap him by arranging review meetings yourself.

– If things are not going well and you are sure that you are under an absolutely bad boss, try to look out for opportunities within the organisation. Don't judge the organisation unfavourably because of your bad experience with one person.

Over-competitive and uncooperative colleagues

Before I get into this discussion, I deem it necessary to discuss a flaw in human judgment system that leads to unfavourable appraisal of those around us. The flaw is called "*Fundamental Attribution Error*". This error can be explained like this:

When a person "A" observes a person "B" making a mistake in a certain situation, person "A" will hold person "B" responsible for it rather than the situation in which person "B" made that mistake. For example if Rohit saw Shobhit unable to drive car properly in bad traffic situation, he would more likely infer that Shobhit is not a good driver rather than inferring that traffic situation might be too bad for even a good driver.

I am different from you. I am a beggar because of my bad luck while you were born to be a beggar.

The fundamental attribution error forces us to judge people unfavourably and discount the role of situations in which other people are acting. And quite contrary to it when people are performing well or are being good, we tend to attribute it to situation or luck. The fundamental attribution error is very strong and it influences unfavourably our appraisal of other people. Quite contrarily when it comes to ourselves, we attribute our failures to situations and luck, while our success to our own ability.

I decided to highlight this effect here in order to make you conscious to the fact that before you judge your colleagues as inherently bad, try to understand the situation in which they are acting. Empathising with your colleagues is often better and a more effective solution than resorting to other solutions that we would discuss here. So before you set out labeling others as difficult people, check the source and approach of your judgment. It might be your own biases or simply envy which make you perceive them in bad light and it actually might be "*You*" who is a "*Difficult*" colleague.

When two or more people work together healthy competition is required to keep the performance improving. It is when the competition exists in absence of trust and cooperation that it becomes toxic for the entire team. It is not uncommon to have a few members in the team who not only try to outdo you every time but may also try to bring your reputation down by indulging in rumour mongering and back-biting. They may also steal ideas and credit. Some of the colleagues might simply be uncooperative. They may not share information, hoard knowledge, documents and be passive when approached. Such colleagues will not do any explicit harm to you but it is still difficult to work with them. Difficult colleagues might also critique you unnecessarily and show total lack of concern for you and others.

Just like bad bosses, bad colleagues also become source of anxiety and stress. In a research[3] conducted by Rob Cross and Robert Thomas, they found that 90% of the anxiety in work comes from 5% of the people you know. So you have to be cautious about those people who have the capability to sap energy out of you.

Let's discuss what you could do for each of these categories of the colleagues:

Free Loaders and Colleagues who would steal credit

Honestly speaking, I have not seen many colleagues in so many years who stole credit for my work. Though, I have heard about a few from my colleagues and friends. Nevertheless, I have seen many who would coast freely with the group without losing anything. Such colleagues don't pull up their own weight and take advantage of the inertial movement that the team provides. It is very difficult to deal with such difficult colleagues and it is still more wearisome when you are a fresher with no prior experience. You need to take some proactive steps to protect yourself from these two types of colleagues.

Often the indications that you are losing credit to someone else are:

- You create a document, do an analysis, make up a proposal, and someone else sends it via email to your boss.
- When it comes to presenting the proposal to your boss or someone else higher up, you don't take up the chance to speak up.
- You are not being marked CC on mails that pertain to work that you are also doing.
- Your roles and responsibilities have not been finalised.

Most of the times colleagues don't steal the credit consciously but when it comes to them they don't deny it either. Ironically many times it is because of non-assertive and naïve behaviours that you put yourself in a situation where you end up losing what you deserve. You need to be conscious of those behaviours of yours that make you prone to losing credit for your work

- First things first, set your roles and responsibilities with your boss. Make sure he knows what are the projects or areas you are handling. Keep him in loop on the progress on each of those goals.
- Whenever you do something that takes significant effort and creativity, inform your boss. Feeling proud of a good job done is not considered bad in organisations. You don't need to be unduly modest about your achievements.
- Remember that you are accountable and answerable to your boss (one who will decide your appraisal rating). If you are sending an important power point presentation, document or something else of importance to a colleague or a senior colleague (who might be your supervisor in a big department), mark a copy to your boss or the HoD. It is ok to be paranoid as long as you are being fair.
- Take opportunities to make presentations and proposals to the higher-ups.

Colleagues who would spread rumours

Spreading rumours about fellow colleagues is an unethical practice that some employees engage in. Most organisations today have well-established whistle blower and anti-bullying or harassment policies. In case you are a victim of a rumour mongering colleague you may use the official channel to handle him. You should not think of taking action at a personal level. If the other person doesn't respect professionalism, you don't need to stoop to his level. Further, you might create problems for yourself by indulging in such an activity yourself.

Colleagues who would horde information and would not support

A colleague who belongs to this category is threatened that you would take his position, would make him redundant, and might steal credit from him. They are generally employees who have spent a lot of time in the organisation and yet have not got recognition in terms of career progression because of lack of educational qualifications or any other reason. If you empathise with such a colleague you will find a person who feels that he has been treated unfairly and has been victimised. You being a new entrant to the system might be perceived by them as a new threat. These people will find it very difficult to trust you with the information that they possesses by virtue of their long association with the organisation. Handling them is actually not difficult if you know how to build trusting relationships. But, that requires some time and a lot of effort. Give them the recognition that they seek so longingly. Spend time talking to them and give importance to their experience, views, and opinions. Make them feel absolutely safe with you. You will find that slowly and gradually the ice will thaw and they will start opening up and will share information with you openly. Remember that you are not there to make competitors but to make colleagues.

Cynical Colleagues

These chronic whiners will have a negative opinion for each and everything that goes on in the organisation. It is very difficult to change such people and if you try to do so, they might actually succeed in winning you to their side (They are more experienced in whining than you are in treating whiners!). The best option when faced with these toxic colleagues is to totally disregard what they say. Talk to them only for professional needs and avoid talking to them as long as possible. However, if because of an unfortunate astrological alignment you are stuck in a conversation with them then you may do best by not adding anything to what they say. Also, don't unnecessarily try to disagree with them. It might exacerbate their complaints and make them combative. Just listen and agree superficially with them. It will soothe their need to vent out and be heard.

Rude and Arrogant Colleagues

Rude and arrogant colleagues are very difficult to approach and can shatter your self-esteem. And, to make the matter a tad bleak, such colleagues are more in number than other types discussed so far. It is almost certain that you will have at least one in your working relationships in the organisation that you join. The key to dealing with these people is being assertive – don't breach their rights but make sure that you don't give away your rights. If there is something that they need to do as part of their official duty – convey it very curtly. Also remember that you can't let your self-esteem suffer because you have been treated as scum by someone else. You get respect only as long as you respect yourself. Don't change your behaviour because of the way they treat you and also don't waste your time thinking about them after you have dealt with them. It is difficult to get favours from these people but get work done from them when they are bound by duty. If a person from this category is very senior and you need to get something done from him, don't hesitate to get your boss in. In any case don't get into arguments with them. Being a fresher you still have a long way to go before people support you if you were to get into an altercation.

Work itself as a source of anxiety and stress

Go around and talk to people how they feel about their work and everyone would have a complaint or two to share. It is difficult to get a work that is absolutely free of anxiety, worry, and stress. As we saw earlier work is supposed to induce some level of stress to keep you moving. Reduced level of anxiety and stress may actually be counter-productive and may result in ennui and boredom. But heightened levels of stress are actually toxic and dangerous. There are a few characteristics related to our work that decide the affective outcomes. But, before I elaborate those outcomes I would like to share a scene from one of the most popular cartoon movies of all times – *Tom and Jerry*.

In one of the episodes, I remember, Tom is chasing Jerry. As Jerry is running for his life on the terrace of a house, he runs into air, not realising that he is past the floor on which he was running. When he does realise his predicament, he looks up and a question mark appears over his head. He grabs the question mark and hooks it on to a cable that he happens to pass by during his free fall. He is saved. Tom, following Jerry, also runs into air and realises his situation when it's quite late. He is also shocked to see the height at which he is stuck without help. His shock and surprise throw up an exclamation mark over his head, which he grabs but which is not as helpful as a question mark with a hook was.

Watching this small scene I realised one bare fact of life. When you are face-to-face with a situation, it is no use being surprised or shocked. It is required in such situations to ask a question – What is that I could do to get the best out of this situation? It is this attitude which differentiates people who succumb to stressful work and those who get the best out of it.

So, we come back to the characteristics of a job that make it inherently stressful to the incumbent.

Skills required to do the job

In case you are insufficiently skilled to do a particular job you would have a low level of self-efficacy which will create apprehension about your growth in the organisation. Whenever you take up a job, be sure that you don't agree to do something that is much beyond your skill level. It is often better to refuse to do something than taking it and ruing later. However, you should not take this as excuse for refusing to do everything. Take an accurate stock of your skills – talk to friends, colleagues, even boss – and then take up tasks that are challenging to an extent where they don't increase stress to dysfunctional level. Remember the inverted curve that we saw earlier – challenge in terms of skill level required should be challenging but not paralysing.

Time available to complete the job

One mistake that people make again and again is making promises that they know they can't keep. Keeping extraordinary situations aside, you should negotiate the time by which you promise to complete the task. If the deadline is already in your face, it would lead to stress and if the deadline is too relaxed it would be too boring. Balance is the mantra.

There is a saying that I would like reiterate here: "Work expands to fill the time available." In order to get maximum out of the 8 hrs of work everyday, it is absolutely essential to manage your time well. In the next chapter we will discuss ways in which you may manage your work and time in the best possible manner.

Perceived control on the outcomes

Research[4] has established that those stressors which we feel less control over have stronger effect on our well-being.

Desire to control our situation and outcomes of our efforts is a basic human need and when it is denied or is perceived to be missing, it results in anxiety and stress. At work you will find that your work is often dependent on a lot of factors that are outside your control. These factors could be: hierarchy, which doesn't allow you to take quick decisions; colleagues in other departments who are outside your influence; non-availability of data for any analysis; or problems that prove too difficult to be solved. Only way to deal with the stress coming out of such things is acceptance of your situation. Certain things in the world can be controlled; some things can be influenced; and, for the remaining you only could have concern. Your task is to understand the difference and accept them as such.

Degree of emotional management required

All of us would like teachers to be patient, policemen to be polite, Air-hostesses to be ever smiling, HR Managers to be servile and so on. We want them to demonstrate just one emotion in all interaction in spite of the situation. Jobs in hospitality and service industry have a typical characteristic that makes them inherently stressful. In these jobs, which have a high degree of customer interface, the employees have to always wear a cheerful and happy demeanour. It becomes very stressful for the employees to display emotions that they are not feeling and is especially worse when they have to maintain a smile on their face and politeness in their tone talking to unhappy or rude customers. It is also difficult to show that you are happy when something back home is not ok. This job requirement, which characterizes such jobs, is called 'Emotional Labour'[5] and is one of the biggest reasons for work related stress. Though it might look like that emotional labour is present only in professions discussed above, it is present in some amount in most of the jobs. Some examples: Pretend to agree with your boss when you don't really; Talk friendly with a colleague who you won't even stand for a second outside office; Working on a project you know will fail; Accepting a negative feedback which you don't agree with and so on. Emotional labour eventually results in burnout and disengagement from work. It's not only the organisation which loses from the effects but the individual too is affected – psychologically and physiologically. To save yourself from the ill-effects of emotional labour it is required that you start learning the art of emotional management, which in itself is a very broad and expansive topic to be covered in one chapter. Research in the area of emotional regulation has suggested several techniques which can be used in reining in disruptive, negative emotions. I am going to share two techniques here with you.

Labeling[6]: Naming your emotion, when it strikes you, brings down the emotion significantly. There is a good amount of research work that is available in support of this fact.

Cognitive Reappraisal[7]: According to the *"Appraisal Theory of Emotions"*, our emotions arise out of our appraisal or interpretation of an event or situation[8]. If our appraisal is negative we suffer from emotions like anxiety, depression, frustration, anger, envy, and jealousy. However, if we could somehow reappraise the situation or the event to be positive or at least non-negative, we may control the arousal of negative feeling and may replace them with positive ones. Cognitive Reappraisal is a cognitive technique in which you try to appraise or understand your situation from a different perspective thereby telling your brain that stress is unwarranted. I would explain this technique using my own experience. My first manager in my first job asked me to start coming in night shifts. I was shocked. Being from one of the premier institutes of the country, I had never thought that I would be going through these abnormal (or, so I thought at that time) things. Night shifts were draining me out. I became quite grubby about the whole thing. Then I realised that coming in night shifts provided me a unique opportunity to sit unperturbed (In a process plant, that too in a maintenance department, most nights often go eventless). I decided to utilise this opportunity to read manuals and other documents in the plant. The knowledge gathered in those sleepless nights came quite handy when I started coming in regular shifts and even after changing my job. I actually reinterpreted the whole event in a way that made me value it rather than despise it. You may find this technique especially useful when you start interpreting difficult situations as opportunities to learn.

In his book **'Your Brain at Work: Strategies for Overcoming Distraction, Regaining Focus, and Working Smarter All Day Long'** David Rock has not only suggested several techniques to managing emotions but has also explained how to leverage the knowledge of neuroscience in improving your effectiveness at work. I highly recommend the book to anyone who is interested in getting the best out of oneself.

Performance Reviews

If there is one thing that is universally dreaded, yet waited for eagerly, in the organisations, it is Performance Review. Organisations often have well defined Performance Management Systems that start from Goal Setting and end up in Performance Appraisals and ratings based on employees' performance. It is the performance appraisal rating that decides their salary increments and promotions. It is because of this critical effect that Performance Review has on employees' overall career progression that it often creates a lot of anxiety in the organisation.

It is possible to reduce this anxiety by being proactive in tracking your goal achievement status and related key

BURN OUT SYNDROME

Burnout Syndrome is a term coined by a Psychoanalyst called Herbert J. Freudenberger after he noticed that his own job changed from rewarding to fatiguing and frustrating over time. Burnout is a state when a person is exhausted mentally and physically after years of toil and stress at professional life. Burnout syndrome usually strikes the best people who don't find it easy to say no to any work assigned to them. Freudenberger et al. divided the development of burnout in 12 phases

1. A compulsion to prove oneself - excessive ambition.
2. Working harder – doing everything, trying to make themselves irreplaceable.
3. Neglecting their needs – not finding enough time for sleeping, eating, socialising, spending time with family.
4. Displacement of conflicts – not being able to relate their inner feeling that something is wrong to the real source.
5. Revision of Values – become blunted emotionally; stress changes their values system.
6. Denial of emerging problems – becoming intolerant, accusing others of being lazy and stupid, not accepting that the problems have emerged because of the way they have changed.
7. Withdrawal – from social contacts; may seek refuse in alcohol or medications.
8. Obvious behavioural changes – becoming fearful, shy and apathetic.
9. Depersonalisation – looking at life mechanically, denying self and others as persons.
10. Inner emptiness – feeling a need to do something relentlessly.
11. Depression – an overpowering feeling of indifferent, hopeless and exhausted.
12. Burnout – mental and physical exhaustion; in need of medical attention immediately.

Source: http://en.wikipedia.org/wiki/Burnout_(psychology)

Exhibit 8.2

performance indicators. As soon as your roles and responsibilities are decided in discussion with your boss, decide on what are the key metrics or measures that would tell you that you are moving towards your goals. Maintain a tracker for your metrics and provide periodical status to your boss (even if he doesn't ask). It is also advisable to keep a diary of your daily work. Keep a list of achievements that you accomplished outside of your routine responsibilities and assigned projects. These documents will form evidence for your achievements and good performance when it is time for the annual appraisal.

By being ready to face it proactively, performance appraisal will hardly be a worry for you.

Anxiety, Worry, and Stress: The Mocking Demons

I would close this chapter by reiterating that undue anxiety and stress is not good for your psychological and physiological health. When body is flooded with stress hormones, all the physical energy is diverted towards preparing body to fight or flight. This means that growth related processes are minimised or halted. Our bodies evolved with this mechanism because survival was more important than growth when our ancestors were face-to-face with a real danger to their life. But, in savannahs, forests and grasslands, our ancestors used to face this type of stress only for a while and not for extended periods. In fact a study[9] of tribal people, who still live a life like our ancestors did, shows that they are outside their caves or groups for not more than 4-5 hrs a day. They spend rest of their time in social activities which help them relax and rejuvenate. It is because of this that our body is ill equipped to deal with extended chronic stress. Chronic stress is really bad for health. Imagine you are a sprinter, as you listen "Ready", "Steady" your body prepares itself for running. Breath and heart rate increase in anticipation of more energy requirement, blood flow increases to muscles, you are all set to run. But if the final "*GO*" never comes, your body remains in the ready to run state. This is what chronic stress is. You anticipate a threat that doesn't come and in its anticipation you play havoc with your own body and mind.

Stress often results in symptoms like loss of sleep, loss of appetite, digestive and gastric troubles, ulcers, and heart diseases. It might also in some cases result in skin ailments like eczema and loss of hair. Besides physiological symptoms it reduces your performance levels and self-esteem. It might result in chronic depression and loss of self-confidence as well. Stress follows a vicious cycle. Once you are into it, you are less strong to face it. And often it becomes difficult to come out. Stress further exacerbates when there is no outlet for frustration, no sense of control, no social support and no hope that situation will improve. One solution that may help pull you out of all these four factors is a good support network of friends and well-wishers. These friends provide you opportunities to vent out frustration, empathise with your concerns, and may help you see the positive side of the situation as well.

Worry, anxiety and stress are because of unfavourable appraisal of events and situations. While other animals push the stress button only when they face real danger, human beings have a tendency to push it at a mere anticipation of danger. Subtle and unreal dangers are often behind the worries and anxieties of our daily lives. A development related feedback from the boss, anticipation of too much work coming your way, a rude colleague, financial and career growth comparisons with peers and friends are enough to trigger the old basic fear and worry in our systems. If you really start thinking and asking questions to yourself about these phantom stressors, they prove to be "mere mocking demons".

Conclusion

Stress and anxiety are an inseparable part of work. While in moderate amount they provide the necessary motivation sustained stress and anxiety can lead to sub-optimal performance and health problems. We have discussed in this chapter several ways in which you may manage stress stemming from different sources. Nevertheless always remember that any technique can be perfected only through practice and same is applicable to the techniques for managing stress also.

CHAPTER 9

Manage Yourself and Your Time

Enter work-life and behold your life's simplicity vanishes into thin air. Goals are no longer stable and independent; they are volatile, complex and interdependent. The complexity of the tasks increases manifold. No longer is it enough to keep in your mind the goals to reach and the tasks to do; try it and you are sure to go mad. Your time is no longer a commodity to which no one but you had claim, here people from all the sides will try to take a chunk of your time. Provided these facts, the business as usual in most organisations is full of inefficiencies and marginal performance.

Though people around might look seriously busy in organisations, they usually remind me of the ancient story of *Sisyphus*. Sisyphus was a Greek King who was punished by the Gods for his hubristic behaviour in a peculiar way. He was given a task of rolling a big boulder up the hill only to see it rolling back and then pushing it back again and again for eternity. The task of Sisyphus was utterly meaningless and unfruitful. In organisations, I am not amazed any more to see, many people are condemned to doing such *Sisyphean* tasks because of their own inability to come out of it and, sadly, because being busy(may be in a fruitless activity) makes them feel important.

It is but very natural for us to attend to tasks which are urgent and which can't be put off to tomorrow. In fact most of us decide our priority list to deal with the urgent task first. The whole futility of this approach is that the list of urgent things keeps on increasing in a vicious fashion. If we only do what is urgent, we would never get time to attend to things that would become urgent tomorrow. It is very easy for one to be driven by urgency factor and doing only what is staring in one's face. The point to realise is that *urgency* is no criteria for prioritisation. It is *importance* rather than *urgency* that should drive our priorities. If you are driven by urgency it is very probable that you roll up the boulder uphill only to find it rolling back on you the next day.

Besides the urgent-important decision being effective at work also requires you to manage yourself in a holistic manner. It is not only time that needs management. You need to manage your physical, spiritual, and mental well-being as well. In this chapter we will learn how you may manage yourself and your time at work and deliver optimum performance.

Long Term Goal Setting

> "Would you tell me, please, which way I ought to go from here?"
>
> "That depends a good deal on where you want to get to," said the Cat.
>
> "I don't much care where~~" said Alice.
>
> "Then it doesn't matter which way you go," said the Cat.
>
> "So long as I get SOMEWHERE," Alice added as an explanation.
>
> "Oh, you're sure to do that," said the Cat, "if you only walk long enough."
>
> **— Alice in Wonderland**

Setting goal is the first thing to do before embarking on a journey. Without deciding on where you want to go you can't choose the direction to move towards. And when you move in any direction you would reach somewhere you didn't intend to go.

Your first task as discussed earlier in the book is to decide your goals in consultation with your boss. You might decide your own learning goals too. Remember the golden rule for deciding the goals – Specific, Measurable, Actionable, Realistic, and Time-bound. For each goal make an action plan with clear and doable activities and timelines. Always remember that a good activity statement has a *verb* in it and answers the question *"How to do it?"* For example if your goal requires you to implement best practices from the industry, one of the activities might be conducting research to identify the best practices. There are two possible activity statements you might use

- Conduct research to identify two best practices from the industry
- Prepare an online survey for identifying best practices and administer to at least 15 different companies.

The first statement is an ongoing activity and doesn't answer the question *"How to conduct the research?"* Looking at the second statement, however, you may realise that it is actually a one-time activity and can be completed in a single attempt. It also tells that the research has to be conducted using a *"survey"*. Chances of completing the second activity are obviously more compared to the first one. You may use the format provided here for making your action plans.

It is also a good idea to indicate the review dates for the activities. Commit yourself to these review dates by blocking your calendar in your e-mail client (outlook or lotus).

Weekly To-do List

Putting in place long term goals provides you a direction in which you need to move. But if you stop at this level of planning, there is more than one obstacle in your way.

- It is probable that some of the goals are easy to achieve and you keep yourself busy doing just the tasks pertaining to them while ignoring other goals.
- The ignored goals keep haunting you creating anxiety. The haunting thoughts also eat up your working memory and leave you less efficient and effective.

153

Table 9.1

GOAL:				TARGET DATE:	
S. No.	Activity	Team Members	Resources Required	Completion Date	Status

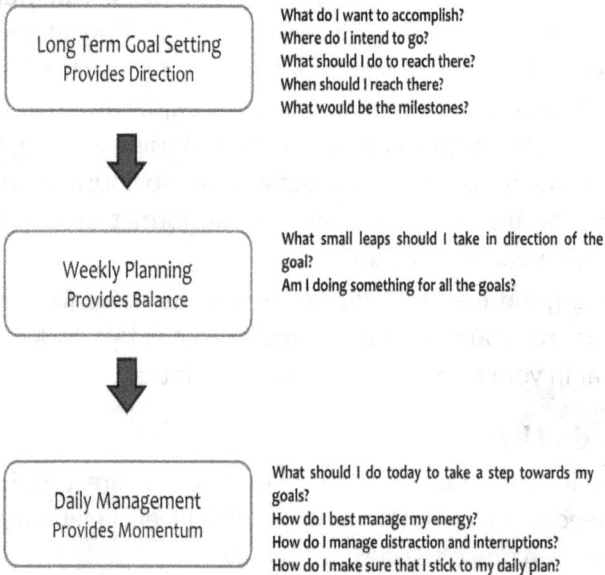

| Long Term Goal Setting
Provides Direction | What do I want to accomplish?
Where do I intend to go?
What should I do to reach there?
When should I reach there?
What would be the milestones? |

| Weekly Planning
Provides Balance | What small leaps should I take in direction of the goal?
Am I doing something for all the goals? |

| Daily Management
Provides Momentum | What should I do today to take a step towards my goals?
How do I best manage my energy?
How do I manage distraction and interruptions?
How do I make sure that I stick to my daily plan? |

Converting Planning Into Action

Figure 9.1

- The resulting confusion because of the above two reasons might lead to demotivation and disillusionment. You might find yourself abandoning your goals altogether.

At the beginning of the week look at all your action plans and pick up action items that are due in that week. Make a to-do list that you would complete in that week. In case a particular activity needs further breaking down into simpler activities, do it. However, make it simpler and no more. This to-do list is still at weekly level and you don't need to break it down to daily level. Remember the rule discussed above. Activities should have a verb and it should answer the question "*How to do it?*" Review this list in the end of the week and update the status. Any uncompleted activity needs to be transferred to the next week's to-do list. Format is provided here.

Table 9.2

	Goal 1	Goal 2	Goal 3	Goal 4
Monday	Activity1		Activity 1	
Tuesday		Activity 1	Activity 2	
Wednesday	Activity 2	Activity 2		Activity 1
Thursday	Activity 3		Activity 3	Activity 2
Friday				Activity 3
Saturday	Activity 4	Activity 3	Activity 4	

Daily Management

Planning takes a lot of mental and intellectual effort. It tells where you are supposed to reach, how you are supposed to reach and when you are supposed to reach there. It also tells what resources will be needed in the endeavour. However, the proof of pudding is in eating. Plans look good and impressive but until they are implemented they are not worth the paper they are written on. And, implementation happens in the live moment; it happens one moment at a time. Day is the unit of time which needs to be managed from hour-to-hour for effective implementation of the plans. If you manage your day, the months and years are automatically taken care of. But this simple truth is so elusive that most of us simply neglect it at our own peril. The elaborate and beautiful plans somehow create the delusion of control which doesn't exist in reality. Managing the day requires deliberate and assiduous efforts to prioritise, to plan to-do items, to deal with interruptions, to avoid procrastinations, and to leverage technology effectively. The rewards of managing the days are big. In a recent book called *THE PROGRESS PRINCIPLE: Using Small Wins to Ignite Joy, Engagement*[1], Amabile and Kramer drew on three decades of research and nearly 12,000 diary entries from more than 200 employees to reveal a telling truth: **Employees' biggest motivator is making consistent, meaningful progress on a daily basis**. In their research they found that people feel more engaged, productive and happy when they make a meaningful achievement that day. So the writing on the wall is: *If you want to live a happy and contended life – go ahead and manage your day to achieve something, however small, every day.*

Prioritising work

Stephen Covey introduced the concept of Second Quadrant Management in his book *7 Habits of Highly Effective People*[2]. The concept highlights that if we should prioritise work based on importance rather than urgency, the number of urgent works will actually reduce. Urgent according to him is something that requires your immediate attention – it could be a report that needs to be sent immediately, a machine breakdown in a plant, ringing phone, unexpected visitor, crises, etc. Important, however, is something that will help you move towards your goal; planning ahead, keeping the track of KRAs, proactively taking feedback from customers, improvement projects, etc. The second quadrant management asks you to focus on not-urgent but important tasks to be able to proactively avoid important-urgent tasks. As Robin Sharma puts it in the book *The Monk who Sold his Ferrari*, you can't be too busy driving that you can't stop for refueling your car. Important things not done on time create urgent crises later.

Exhibit 9.1

How no prioritisation could spoil daily management

Rohit reached offi ce, as usual, 15 minutes late. The traffi c in the city is too bad and Rohit stays too fa away from the offi ce. However he might try, it seemec impossible to reach office in time. He thanked God that his organisation didn't take late coming too seriously and he could make it up by staying 15 minutes late in the evening. He started his computer and opened the inbox. Most of the people had already reached and his inbox had already received quite a few mails. He opened the mails one after another. "There are too many things coming my way", he thought, "How on earth do they think that I can do so many things?" There was one specific mail that caught his attention. He had sent a mail previous evening to Amit and without checking that mail he had sent a stinker mail to Rohit. It was very infuriating. "These people have gone stupid", he thought again. He had a few urgent things left from previous evening. He tried to recollect what they were. He wrote them down on a piece of paper. First thing to be completed was to analyse the customer feedback for the previous months and send a report indicating actions points. As he started the analysis, his thought kept going back to Amit's mail. He stopped in between and wrote back to Amit asking him to check his mails properly before writing to others. He started doing the analysis again, when he realised that he had a meeting to attend in a short-while. "The report is definitely going to be delayed this time. I think I should stop checking my mails in the morning. They might be too distracting and energy draining", he thought and left for the meeting.

This is a really good approach to prioritising your work on a weekly or a monthly basis. But, yet, it would not tell you how to prioritise your to-do list on a daily basis. Each work that you do draws a different type of energy[3] – mental, physical, and emotional. These energies though different from each other are interdependent and affect each other. They have to be utilised in a way that results in optimum output.

Mental Energy is needed for works that need you to focus, pay attention and process information. We had discussed earlier in the book that part of the brain responsible for this type of work is limited in nature, guzzles a lot of energy and gets exhausted easily. This part of the brain is also easily distracted by physical and emotional discomforts. So, it is but imperative that when you make your to-do list, plan to do this type of work in the very beginning of the day, when your brain is still brimming with energy and is not exhausted. Some examples of such work: Data analysis, Writing, Preparing Presentations, Reading reports or manuscripts, any other creative work, etc. As seen in the example in the box – checking emails is an energy draining exercise and should not be done as the first thing in the morning. It is best if emails are checked after your most important works are finished. **Roy F. Baumeister,** a professor of psychology, and author of the book *Willpower: Rediscovering the Greatest Human Strength*, told in an interview[4] that most productive people do their best work early in the day. He also underscores the importance of having a good healthy breakfast before starting your day.

Getting work done through others is a task that invariably uses up the emotional energy. Persuading others, making a sales pitch, giving feedback, receiving feedback, doing repetitive and monotonous job, showing emotions that you don't feel are some activities that are part and parcel of the daily life. These activities often leave you exhausted emotionally and thus mentally. If you drain yourself emotionally in the beginning of the day, it is difficult to focus on things that require your quality attention (mental energy). Further, emotional drainage may also leave you more irritable and less patient and tolerant. Such tasks therefore should be prioritised after those which require mental energy but not immediately after. The structure of the brain is such that usage of mental energy also reduces the capacity to manage emotions. After mental effort it takes a while to replenish its stock of energy and be ready for next job. It is therefore advisable to sandwich some break between the two. A small trip to the cafeteria, walk to water-cooler and a small talk with a colleague may do the trick.

One more type of energy which is usually utilised in low-end work is Physical Energy. This is the energy which is utilised while doing physical work. In the beginning of your career you might be assigned a lot of administrative work. For completing this type of work you might have to run around doing errands, take printouts, travel within the city during office hours. Physical energy when drained diminishes the supply of mental energy, yet it is useful in dissipating negative emotional energy and revitalising oneself. These types of work therefore are best done as last thing in the day. But, you may also club some of it in between mental and emotional works.

Planning the day keeping in mind the energy requirements lets you get the most out of your day.

Writing Effective To-do lists

At daily management level, things need to be done one step at a time. Each step is a short activity that could be done and completed in one go. If you were to write it down, it will be defined with specific action verb e.g. write, call, talk, meet, list-down, etc. This activity should be as granular as possible. While making your to-do list these things have to be kept in mind. Taking the same example that we used earlier – in case your long term object is to design and conduct survey for identifying best practices in the industry, you should not write an action item like – "Work on designing the survey". The action item should be more specific like – "Write down the possible questions for the survey" or "Fix a meeting with XYZ for vetting the survey questions". Once you have written down the activities arrange them in the priority as per the principles discussed earlier. Writing to-do list helps you keep to-do things out of your mind and hence frees up your brain to do other more value adding and creative things. It also is an excellent tool to keep your morale high. As you complete small tasks a feeling of achievement comes that keeps your spirits high. According to the book *The Enthusiastic Employee*[5] feeling of achievement is one of the three factors that keep enthusiasm of an employee high. Enthusiasm is a desirable characteristic not only for the company alone; employee's overall well-being, including physiological and psychological well-being, also depends on his level of enthusiasm towards life.

Handling Interruptions

Writing to-do list is one thing and making sure that you stick to that is another. There are a lot of possible interruptions that occur throughout the day to distract and make you compromise with your plan. Even a small interruption is enough to increase significantly the time taken to finish the work[6], sometimes up to 50%, because it takes time to come back to the same state of mind where you left the work. Interruptions also similarly increase the chances of errors by diverting your focus from the task at hand. Moreover, it is very difficult to get riddance from interruptions because we live and work in an environment designed for interruptions – *phone calls, SMSs, emails*; and, you thought it is only people who interrupt you. While technology is supposed to increase our productivity it actually ends up reducing it by creating a felt need to be interrupted every now and then. In fact people are addicted so much these days to email and phone that they really have an obsessive need to check phone and email continually. The advent of smart phones, laptops, tablets has only worsened the situation. According to Basex[6], an IT research and consulting firm, an average information worker — anyone who works on a desk — loses 2.1 hours of productivity every day to interruptions and distractions. The first thing to avoid interruption thus is to get disconnected for the time you are busy doing something that needs your full attention. Put your phone on silent mode and change the setting in your mail client to remove notification of new mail arrivals. You may set aside specific time to check your emails and reply all in one go. It is easier said than done for experienced people but for freshers who are yet to acquire these bad habits, I would suggest, adopt this ritual of setting aside a specific time for checking emails and messages and never acquire the obsessive need to be in touch continuously.

Besides technology there are some universal interruptions that vie for your attention and disrupt the flow of your work. It is important that we discuss how to handle those interruptions as well.

- Some Colleagues drop by to say hello and initiate discussions that have the potential to take more time than you could spare. In case you are busy with an important work it becomes very difficult to ask such people to go for the sake of courtesy. To diplomatically handle this situation, adopt a body posture that indicates that you are not ready to leave your work. When such a person happens to come to your workstation, don't leave your work completely. Keep your hands on your keyboard or on the paper (in case it is a paperwork you are doing). Most people are sensitive enough to understand this tacit signal and leave soon. But in case the person is more tenacious, you may leave your seat and stand. Don't sit and talk. This may encourage the other person to grab a chair and sit. Once he sits it is probable that he will take unduly more time. If the person still doesn't leave, then you leave making an excuse to go to rest-room or some meeting.

- If it is your boss who decides to interrupt you with some urgent work, it is *ok* to share that you are busy and would be able to deal with next thing after you are through with the current assignment. It is better to be straightforward and say *no* rather than taking on work that you know will get delayed.

- If someone wants to meet you, it is better to go to his/her place rather than asking him/her to come to yours. First benefit: You get some physical exercise. Second benefit: You may decide when to leave.

- Unexpected visitors may also drop-by sometimes. These might be vendors, suppliers or even customers who decide to visit you for courtesy sake when they come near your office for some other purpose. In official circles, it is not considered offensive if you explain your inability to meet someone due to your busy schedule. Don't let someone visit you if you feel that you don't really have time available. Thanks them for calling, tell them upfront about your inability to meet them and apologise sincerely. Make it a principle to meet people only through appointment.

- Searching for misplaced things is another major interruption and time eater. Say you are writing a mail in which you need to make a reference to a memo that you received the previous day. Somehow you placed it somewhere you don't remember now. Finding the memo is going to waste precious time and is also going to exasperate you. Despite this obvious loss because of misplaced things most of us don't take organising our work place seriously. Before you leave your desk every day, make sure that your desk is clean. Throw away each and every paper that is not going to be of any help in future. You would be amazed to realise how clean and clutter free your desk would become just by throwing away useless stuff.

- Similar to misplacing physical things, is misplacing electronic information. I have seen many people just don't deem it necessary to organise the files in their computers. They store everything either on the desktop or in one of the disk drives without any logic. Though computers come with search function, it still saves time if you have made appropriate folders and have stored files where they belong. Naming files itself may help you save time. When you make several versions of a same document, it doesn't help to name it "Document_Latest", because afterwards everything becomes old (doesn't remain latest ever). It is advisable to add date of revision in the name of the document so that you know later the date of final edit. Similarly make appropriate folders in your email inbox as well.

Avoiding procrastination

"That which you ignore
Will rise up and strike you."
—Performance artist; Jenny Holzer

Procrastination is one sin (one among many) that I am guilty of. Writing here how to tackle it feels a tad hypocritical to me. But, I have been fighting with it assiduously and I believe that one day I would be able to get good riddance of this really bad habit. I know that I am not alone who is guilty of procrastination and I have a really good company. According to one research 95% people procrastinate at least occasionally and 15-20% of adults routinely (Piers Steel) and habitually procrastinate[7] (At this point I actually decided that I should write the remaining part of this chapter the next morning. Procrastination, you are such a demon!)

According to Piers Steel there are three reasons for procrastination

1. Expecting too little: If you think that there are less chances that you would succeed in your task, it creates a sort of uneasiness and anxiety in your mind. This

uneasiness and anxiety make you defer the work to a later date as you don't yet feel ready to face failure or rejection.

2. Devaluing the task: Tasks that are routine and basic are at the peril of being ignored and pushed aside for future. Paying the bills, giving car for maintenance, health check-up, are some activities that are basic and routine but still very important. Many people are absolutely at ease in procrastination of these tasks.

3. Deferred Gratification: This is no secret that we run after immediate gratification. Things that provide immediate gratification are more tempting than those which require sustained and diligent effort for an extended period of time. Such tasks thus are put off to a later date.

Psychologists appear to be very theoretical and nerdish but these people have devised so many practical techniques for our routine lives that you would be amazed to learn them. I am going to share with you one such technique here. I have found this technique absolutely amazing and very powerful in vanquishing procrastination. This technique proposed by a Psychologist named Peter Gollwitzer is called "Implementation Intention[8]".

When you decide to achieve something you develop "Goal Intention". Goal intention, however, is not sufficient to push you enough to achieve it. In fact Peter Gollwitzer says that it can explain only up to 15-20% of goals achieved. It is because we mostly fail even to initiate the goal directed behaviours because of several reasons: Firstly, there might be conflict between different ways of doing the thing; secondly, the situations which might offer an opportunity to implement action might be habitually used for other non-productive purposes; thirdly, such opportunities might miss our attention all together. *Implementation Intention* helps you initiate actions in situations that have an opportunity of moving towards goal attainment. The first step towards establishing an implementation intention is to identify those opportunities. Say, I have to complete a report and my office schedule is completely tied up for the following day. I have one opportunity that may help me complete it; by starting early from home I may save travel time and complete my report in the early hours at office when my schedule is free. Once you have identified the opportunity decide what exactly you would do to leverage that particular opportunity. So, I know that to reach office early I need to get up early in the morning. "Getting up early in the morning" thus becomes my implementation intention.

Implementation intention means deciding a series of *if-then* statements that make your responses to external stimuli automatic. In previous example, "if schedule is tight, then get up and reach office early" is the implementation intention.

I used to have a more fundamental problem however: How to get up early? Implementation intention helped me there as well. When alarm rang, I had a tendency to put it on snooze or put it off for good to steal a few more moments of sleep. So I had an implementation intention established to tackle this problem as well. I decided – if alarm rings, then I get up and wash my face. This implementation intention though looks so simple has proved so powerful for me that since the day I established it my success rate of getting up in the morning at will has increased significantly. In absence of this implementation intention I went by the automatic response of pushing the snooze button, but with the intention established my brain had other command as well and it went by that.

You may identify opportunities where you tend to indulge in procrastination and decide what is that you will do when you find yourself in those situations. Some examples are given below

-   If you find yourself procrastinating for fear of failure, then seek help from your boss.
-   If you find yourself procrastinating because the task is boring, then decide to reward yourself with a treat immediately after completing it.

- If you find yourself procrastinating because of need to socialise or nibble on snacks, then close yourself in a meeting room or a discussion hall and complete your work. (If you still work on a desktop, don't whine – arrange for a laptop)

- Don't leave your to-do tasks on a list without assigning to them the specific time at which you will do them. Research[9] has proved that if you decide when and where you would do a certain thing, then it increased the chances of your actually doing it by more than 300%.

Implementation intention provides you alternatives to your basic and more automatic responses to environmental stimuli and thereby presents an opportunity to trump them.

Myth of Multitasking

As you enter the field of work, it is possible that you find yourself inundated with various demands pulling you in different directions. Such pressures coupled with the *24x7* connectivity through emails, smart-phones and likes would force you to multi-task. It means that you might find yourself in situations where you are talking on the phone while writing an email to a colleague, or working on an excel sheet while stopping to check a new mail, or juggling between different tasks at the same time. Till quite recently multitasking had been supposed to be a desirable trait in an employee. Organisations had accepted the fact that it is not possible to live without multitasking in a world as busy as today. This was the state of affairs till recently psychologists found that multitasking is a myth. Human brain is designed to deal effectively only with one thing at a time. When you try to do more than one thing at a time, your brain gets slower and less accurate. It's for the same reason that it is illegal to talk on phone while driving. Remember the queer characteristic of brain which provides it limited capacity to pay attention, hold information in working memory and control emotions. Multitasking, according to a research, can reduce your IQ more than Marijuana[10]. Paying attention to one thing at a time is the tip that most successful people follow. When you try doing several things at a time you take more time than working one at a time. Multitasking is not an effective way of doing things that require your attention. If you really want to do two things at a time, make sure that at least one of the things is as automatic for you as breathing.

Conclusion

In order to achieve best performance from your brain and body, you need to keep them in a perfect shape. Listen keenly to your physiological cues and provide rest and replenishment when required. In fact human body works best when periods of intense work are followed by brief periods of rejuvenation. According to Tony Schwartz, an ideal period of intense work should be 90 minutes. You should then break for a small walk, snack and even a nap. Don't try to treat your body like a machine. It was never designed for constant duty. Try not to work on weekends and late into evenings. Do regular physical exercise, eat healthy food, read books, pursue a hobby, talk to friends, and watch a movie once in a while. Life is short, don't get old in office. Always remember that livelihood is just a mean not the end.

Understanding Organisations

Organisations are like individuals. They have growth spurts like kids, mature with time, get old and eventually die. No organisation will last forever. Like individuals they have different values, beliefs, strengths and weaknesses. They have a character that is unique to them. However, unlike individuals organisations are socio-technical entities and have different processes interacting with each other. For an individual who hopes to survive in a given organisation, it is imperative to understand and adapt to these processes. In this section we will discuss: What is an organisation? How are organisations structured? What are different typologies of organisation culture? And, what are different processes operating in an organisation?

CHAPTER 10

Organisations: Structure, Culture, and You

If there is one thing that has not stopped intriguing me, since I started working almost a decade ago, is the nature of organisations. When I think of organisations, the images that conjure up in front of my eyes are those of a machine, a family, a battle ground, and a live organism. And, when I think deeply I find that organisations are none of them and all of them, at the same time. They produce goods and services like machines; they have people, who have a sense of belongingness to each other and the organisation, like a family; they are full of politics, gossips, competition, envy, jealousy, and intrigues like battle grounds; and finally, they grow, respond to threats, have values and beliefs, have individual characters, like living organisms.

Why Care About Organisation Structure and Culture?

Organisations are not new for any of us. You would have been part of so many organisations. Schools, Colleges, Clubs, Societies are nothing but organisations. You should be thinking: "If I have seen and been a part of organisations, why is it now necessary to learn afresh about them?" Business organisations are different from the organisations that we have just mentioned. In business organisations you work for the organisation's sake, but in earlier organisations, it was organisation that worked for you. This fact doesn't imply that organisation theories are different for these types of organisations; it does imply that your survival in business organisations depends a great deal on how much you understand them. As a new entrant to organisational life, it would help you if you know: How organisations are structured? What are different processes in a typical organisation and how they interrelate? What are some typologies of organization structure? However, working in an organisation, whose character differs significantly from yours, is time and energy wasted. It might push you into despair, pessimism and depression. If this mismatch happens to be in your first job then it might lead to loss of self-esteem and self-efficacy – which certainly are not right signs for career progression. To avoid such a scenario you need to understand different types of organisations in terms of structure and culture and then decide which one matches with your own type.

Organisation Structure

Organisations are made of people. People who carry out different roles and responsibilities based on their specialties, competencies, and experience levels. These different people are supposed to work together towards bigger organisational objectives which can be achieved only when there is some sort of structured coordination among them. In smaller organisations this coordination is achieved through one-to-one interactions. Smaller organisations thus have a very loose structure or no structure at all. But as an organisation grows, it becomes more difficult to coordinate this way. Organisations thus develop a structure to cater to the need of coordination in a more complex environment.

Organisation structure helps in bringing coordination in the organisation through division of labour, delegation of power, distribution of resources and flow of command through bureaucracy. It also acts along with organisation culture to affect the way the employee interacts with the organisation, takes decisions, is motivated and rewarded, is made to learn, and is influenced and changed if need be.

Organisation design theory is wide and broad and there are different ways in which organisation structures can be defined. In this book I would discuss five organisation structures as defined by Henry Mintzberg[1]. These structures have been very simply and elegantly explained by Mintzberg. According to him, a typical organisation has the following components

1. Operating core: It consists of people directly involved in production of goods or services – Technicians, Customer Service Executives, Engineers, Supervisors, etc.

2. Strategic Apex: It consists of people who decide on the direction in which the organisation is supposed to move. They are answerable to the stakeholders of the organisation. For example – CEO, CFO, Senior General Managers, etc.

3. Middle Line: This stratum consists of people who connect the operating core to the strategic apex. They have formal authority to get work done from the operating core – Head of Departments.

4. Techno-structure: These are control analyst who design the work flow, plan it, change it or train the people who do it, but they don't do it themselves. For example – Industrial Engineers, Quality Assurance and Quality Control Professionals etc.

5. Support staff: These are specialised units that support the organisation from outside its work-flow, eg. Admin department, HR department etc.

These components have a propensity to pull the organisation in one of the directions. Strategic Apex represents power so it pulls the organisation towards centralisation; Middle line requires formal authority so it pulls the organisation towards divisionalisation or balkanisation where they could run

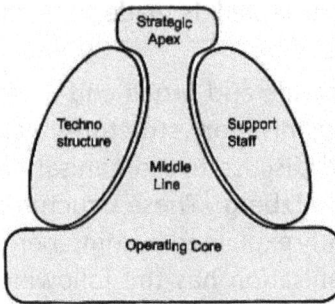

Figure 10.1

their own small organisations; Techno structural components pulls towards standardisation of work and output; Support staff pulls towards collaboration; and the operating core pulls the organisation towards professionalisation where they could have increased autonomy in their work. Based on the relative sizes of these five components there are five types of organisation structures. In describing these structures their related culture, I am not restraining myself to Henry Mintzberg and am adding observations from my own experience of a little less than 100 organisations that I interacted with during my tenure with Confederation of Indian Industry.

Simple Structure

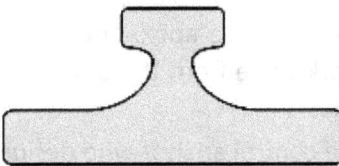

Figure 10.2

As the name suggests, these organisations are very simple in structure. The strategic apex directly directs and supervises the operating core. The middle line is either missing or limited and there is not techno-structure component. Such organisations are usually found in young entrepreneurial organisations and old family run businesses which didn't have gumption enough to grow beyond certain size. They are simple but maybe hostile and aggressive (in young and entrepreneurial cases). Hierarchy may exist but it doesn't provide power and authority, which depend on how near, personally, an employee is to the center of power – nearer he is, more powerful he becomes. Trustworthiness and loyalty are valued more than talent and expertise in these organisations. One clear advantage that this structure has is that decision making is fast as there are fewer layers to get through. Though, the decision making power is usually reserved with the leader. As there are not many people to be managed in this structure coordination is usually through direct one-to-one interactions. The leader at the top of the *strategic apex* leads by charisma or coercion. Further, such organisations are small in size and operations; they can't afford to keep specialists and experts. They need people who are ready to do whatever it takes to achieve the goals of the organisations.

Chances are usually less that you end up in such an organisation unless you decide to join a start-up organisation – for old, small size family run organisations don't believe in recruiting fresh graduates without experience. People who can adapt successfully to such organisations must

- Be able to empathise and understand what the strategy apex requires.
- Be good in interpersonal relationships and build trusting relationships with leaders
- Accept being without structured and well defined roles and responsibilities and be flexible enough to accomplish things based on the emergent requirements
- Be willing to subdue to authority
- Be ready to accept a system without meritocracy

Machine Bureaucracy

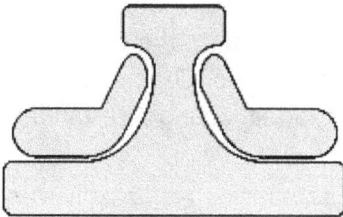

Figure 10.3

You would encounter this type of organisations quite often. Formalised procedures, highly specialised but repetitive and routine operating task, a sharp distinction between line and staff, well defined roles and responsibilities, standard operating procedures, obsession with control – are some of the characteristics of a Machine Bureaucracy. Coordination in Machine Bureaucracy is achieved by standardisation of operations, processes and quality of the final outcome. When you go to a McDonald outlet anywhere in the country, you will not be amazed to see the consistency in the way they operate and obviously almost standard taste of the Burgers that you eat. It is because of standardisation of processes and procedures. You would find this structure in organisations which exist in simple, stable and predictable environment.

The groups are made within these organisations based on functions; roles and responsibilities are clearly defined and deviance is not considered lightly. Here, you will also find a lot of initiatives like TQM, Six Sigma, ISO, and other quality certifications. They pride themselves in producing goods and services with high precision again and again. You find such structures in most manufacturing and service firms – Textile, Cement, Telecom, and Automobile etc.

Decisions are made in these organisations based on defined "Delegation of Power". Smaller decisions are made quickly but bigger and more critical decisions take a long of time in getting through. These organisations thus are not very good in responding to dynamic environment. Hierarchy here is an absolute and people derive their authority out of it. Though experts are also respected in these organisations, they value practicality over academics. They recruit people with a set of special skills and then expect them to acquire expertise in whatever they do. In my experience of such organisations, they don't discourage innovation all together; they believe in small and gradual improvements over time. Change in these organisations is effected through gradual change in standard operating processes and procedures.

For the employees, these organisations are usually very equitable and reward them based on their performance. Because roles, responsibilities, and performance metrics are clearly communicated, these organisations are characterised by meritocracy. You can go as far up as your talent could take you.

But, the danger here is narrow development – because of their emphasis on improving efficiency through expertise. For people who wish to gain expertise in a single function, these are very opportune places to learn, develop and grow. However, these could be very boring places for extrovert, young, and restless people who value change over acceptance.

For thriving in these organisations, you must

- Be steady and consistent
- Be willing to gain expertise in a single function. Broad based development is rarely possible here.
- Be able to improve the system gradually; they value improvement (though gradual)
- Be conformant and compliant
- Be ok with routine and repetitive work pattern
- Be tolerant of tall hierarchy

Professional Bureaucracy

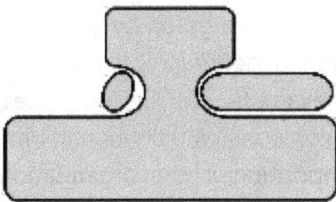

This type of structure is found in schools, colleges, hospitals, law-firms, consultancies etc. where the expertise of the operating core is made up of highly trained professionals. The bureaucracy here is achieved through

Figure 10.4

standardisation of skills. The operating core operates relatively free from the administrative hierarchy and even colleagues. They are autonomous in the way they carry out their work as long as they don't pose a danger to the interests of the organisation. Because the work is complex, the techno-structure component is smaller; it is difficult to standardise complex work which requires improvisation and innovativeness.

The decision making is fast because of autonomy entrusted with the operating core. It is a system of meritocracy and the employee's performance can be easily seen and appraised in isolation. They usually recruit people based on their professional qualifications and training. A lot of money is spent on employees to keep them updated with the latest.

To be successful in this type of an organisation structure, you must

- Have a good professional qualification from a good institute
- Be innovative and creative in your approach. Break-through ideas are encouraged and rewarded in these organisations
- Be able to work independently and take complex decisions independently
- Have good communication and interpersonal skills

Divisionalised firm

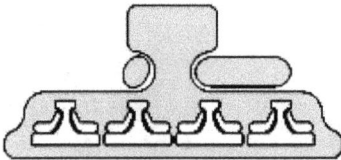

Figure 10.5

This type of structure emerges in organisations that are charac-terised by multiple products or service offerings or by presence in varied geographical locations, for example FMCG companies, Conglomerates, Multinational Firms etc. It is nothing more than a superimposition of other organisation structures. In order to solve the problem of multiplicity, the entire firm is divided into divisions based on products, services or geography. This helps the organisation to ensure fast and contextual decision making through decentralisation of power to divisions.

The pertinent question here for you is – What is the structure in the divisions themselves? Once you have this answer, you may read earlier description to get answers to other relevant questions.

Adhocracy

While bureaucracies are characterised by control through standardisation, adhocracies derive their functionality from flexibility, innovation and creativity. It is suffice to say that adho-

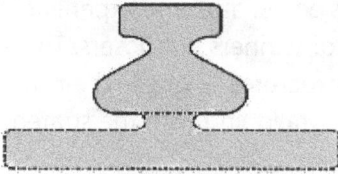

Figure 10.6

cracies have no defined structure that it will stick to. Their prime focus is to solve a particular problem in a unique way with whatever resources they have. People are moved around and assigned to problems – based on their expertise and skills and the requirement. Many organisations which could otherwise be professional bureaucracies exist as adhocracies if they don't stick to categorising teams. An adhocratic approach is eclectic and desultory. Adhocracy is the best way to deal with dynamism and complexity together. If you were to survive in such an organisation you should

- Be highly flexible
- Be highly qualified and talented
- Be ready to work without defined roles and responsibilities
- Have problem solving skills
- Be task oriented rather than routine
- Be a good team player
- Be empathetic for the customer or client

Different personalities suit to different organisation structures. If you are in a structure that doesn't suit your personality, chances of your getting frustrated are very high. However, I am really a big admirer of the adaptability of human beings. All organisations have different personalities of people and they do rather *ok* even in structures and cultures that are quite unlike them. But, then there is a difference between people who do rather ok and those who outshine others. Charles Handy in *Gods of Management*[2] draws a similarity between his model of organisation cultures and four types of personalities proposed by Michael Maccoby in his book *The Gamesman the New Corporate Leaders*[3]. I will try to correlate these personality types with the organization structures we just studied. The four types proposed by *Maccoby* are:

The *Jungle Fighter*, whose goal is power and who experiences life and work as a jungle, a game of winners and losers. These people would do well in Simple structures – where there is a chance to assume absolute power by aligning with the strategy apex.

The *Company Man*, whose sense of identity is based on being a part of the powerful protective company. They are steady and are concerned with the human side of the organisations. They are also committed to the organisations integrity; they are conformists and conscientious. This type might do well in Machine Bureaucracy because of the inherent stability and predictability in that structure. I also think that Simple Structure with a Benevolent Autocrat as the leader may also provide a suitable place for this type.

The *Gamesman*, is characterised by a sense of competition, creativity, innovation, problem solving and team work. These people are sure to belong to Professional Bureaucracy and to some extent to adhocracy.

The *Craftsman*, is one who enjoys creating new things. He derives his satisfaction from utilising his skills to the optimum level. He is more concerned with creativity than anything else. Such people would do rather well in Adhocracies and Professional Bureaucracies. The repetitive nature of Machine Bureaucracy may bore them and subjugation to power in Simple Structure may threaten them. They are free birds; professionals before employees.

The descriptions above may guide you to the type of organisation you naturally belong.

Socio Processes in Organisations

Organisations above all are groups of people who come together to achieve common objectives. Provided this, it is easy to see that organisations must be social entities that have rationality and technicality superimposed over them. We saw in earlier discussion various ways in which organisations are structured to achieve their objectives. We also discussed how different structures put different expectations on their members – but in all this we missed to see that whatever way an organisation is structured there still is something that remains the same: *Social System*. And, like all social systems this one also is concerned with three issues[4]:

- Issues of sustenance and survival
- Issues about ordering and organising
- Issues about purpose, identity, rituals, values and beliefs

It is important to understand the socio-processes going on behind the technical façade of the organisation in order to comprehend the organisation behaviour and behaviour of those working in them. Sometimes mere rationalising behaviours is enough to help you assuage negative feelings emerging out of futile sense making exercise that newcomers indulge in on joining a new organisation.

I came across the model, which I am going to use to explain the socio process, in the Facilitative Leadership Workshop conducted by Institute of Cultural Affairs, Australia. This model is called Social Process Triangles. This model was developed in preparation for a Research Assembly put on by the *Ecumenical Institute* in Chicago, Illinois in 1971, and then has been adapted in several forms by several organisations. I found this model extremely powerful in understanding an organisation. It is a comprehensive model which lets you see three different processes going on simultaneously in an organisation: *Economic* (survival and sustenance), *Political* (Ordering and Organising), and *Cultural* (Purpose, Rituals, and Values and Beliefs).

I am going to adapt this model here to present before you a structured approach to understand organisations as social communities.

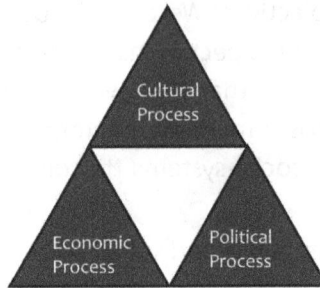

SOCIO PROCESSES IN ORGANIZATIONS

Figure 10.7

Economic Process

This is the foundation process of any organisation; without this the organisation will not serve any purpose and would possibly not exist at all. It tells you:*What does the organisation do for sustenance?* It deals with utilising resources, producing goods and then distributing or selling them to those who require those goods. The goods might as well be services. To understand this process you need to ask these questions

- What do we produce – goods and/or services?
- Who are our customers?
- What are the resources we use to serve our customers – technological, natural, and human? Who provides those resources? At what cost? Who decides the price?
- What are the concerns regarding resources – demand and supply?
- Are their technical instruments and machinery required for production/service? What are those?
- What are the technical processes in converting the resources into goods/services?
- What are the management practices?
- What type of employees are employed – specialists, common laborers, Knowledge workers, general supervisors?

The answers to these questions are explicit and relatively easy to find. In fact, most organisations have answers to these questions in documented form.

Political Process

The word political has negative connotations. Here this word is not used in normal pejorative sense; but in a very literary sense. It includes those processes that help in ordering and organising in order to prevent chaos. It answers a very important question: *How does the organisation does what it does*? It talks about organisation structure, rules, procedures, hierarchy, decision making process, governance and control.

It is a very important process to understand. If you don't understand this then you are up for more than one problem. Firstly, in absence of this knowledge your effectiveness will suffer; you would grope in dark for finding the right way of getting things done. Secondly, you might take decisions that are against the normal ways of the organisation; your conduct in this case will be questioned. Despite this importance, not all organisations would have answers to all these questions in a written explicit format. As we saw in the discussion of organisation structures, in simple structure and in adhocracy these questions are usually left unanswered and decisions are taken often at the moment when the problem arises. In such cases the process is largely tacit.

For learning about the explicit part of this process, you may ask a few simple questions

- What is the organisation structure?
- What is the hierarchy?
- How is power delegated? Is there a written document?
- Where can I get the HR Policy handbook?
- Is there a Governance Policy? If yes, where can I get it?
- What is the performance management process in the organisation?

- What are my roles and responsibilities? Would I have a documented goal sheet? When will it be reviewed? Who will review it?
- Are there councils and committees existing in the organisation? What do they discuss and decide?
- What are the employment laws applicable?
- What are the welfare policies?
- How is salary and job fitment done?
- How is information shared?

However, it is the tacit part which is more difficult to fathom. To tackle this there is no well proven strategy but I would still suggest a few that I found working in my experience.

- What are the stories that people tell? Of success, of failures, of conflicts, of achievements. Listen to them carefully and analyse them. Find answers to these questions:
  - If there was a proposal involved, who proposed and who approved?
  - If there was a decision taken, what were the criteria that were considered? Who took the decision? Was it taken at the operator level, middle level, or the leadership level? Who were the stakeholders?
  - If there was a resource allocation done, who controlled it?
  - If groups and team were formed, how were the groups formed? Who led the team – specialist or generalist?
  - What are some of the priorities consistently shown while making decisions?
  - If there was a conflict, how was it resolved? Who resolved it?
  - Finally integrate all those answers to answer this question - What are some of the behavioural guidelines that you may cull out of the stories for yourself?

- Observe how proposals are made and approved. Are approvals taken verbally or in written? Are their Inter-office-Memos sent across for various approvals or emails are enough?
- Ask the office boy about what files are maintained in the organisation? What should be documented and what not?
- And, finally, be a keen observer.

Cultural Process

Economic process that deals with sustenance and survival is always at tension with the Political process which defines how things are to be done. This tension is inherent because economic process concerns only with goals, in pursuit of which anything can be done. But doing anything to achieve the goals may lead to conflicts and chaos. Political process comes to rescue and puts a rein on those who drive the economic process by binding them with controls thereby creating resistance and tension in addition to order. It is the cultural process that provides a way to manage this tension and make the entire system functional. Cultural process provides social commonality to people coming together to form the organisation. It provides them a meaning and purpose of existence by combining economic struggle with political orderliness. This process describes some fundamental existential questions pertaining to interpreting the collective knowledge; organising the collective norms, rituals, mores, values, and beliefs; and symbolising the collective life and achievements. Understanding this part of the socio-process is the most difficult one because a big part of collective knowledge is tacit, almost all of norms, rituals, mores, values are abstract, and quite certainly symbols are – well – symbolic. Moreover, it is this process that a new comer to the organisation must get adapted to in order to function well. In some studies conducted in last decade, researchers found that lack of knowledge of culture is very common among recent graduates and that they also believed that it is negatively correlated with the socialisation process[5]. The feeling of groupness that members of an organisation feel is because of shared experiences and emotions that they encounter together[6]. As they keep discussing or celebrating these experiences they start identifying themselves with the larger group – which also has same experience as they as individuals have. A newcomer coming to the organisation is instinctively considered a foreigner and an alien (Evolutionary reasons: A person coming from outside the tribe was treated as a foe unless he proved otherwise). Human beings instinctively thwart endeavors of those who they don't consider part of their group. As long as the new comer doesn't share a commonality in culture with the others, he would get a treatment of an alien and would not get the membership to the organisation.

Understanding Collective Knowledge

Collective knowledge in an organisation could be explicit, documented and articulated; or, implicit, embedded in the collective consciousness of the organisation. We dealt with most of the explicit knowledge in our discussions of economic and political processes but left implicit knowledge largely untouched. Implicit knowledge forms when the organisation faces challenges and overcomes them as a whole. Such challenges and experiences help them identify what works and what doesn't work in their environment. In order to gain this knowledge you need to –

- Read or hear the history of the organisation
- Analyse the challenges that the organisation has faced.
- Cull out the learning that the organisation had from facing those challenges.

Many organisations these days have started formally capturing such experiences. They also make conscious efforts to share them with the members through Knowledge Management initiatives. It helps them percolate the culture down.

This part of the learning happens gradually if you don't make any effort. However, through a conscious effort you may settle down in the organisation very soon. And sooner you do that sooner you become productive.

Exhibit 10.1

Language – An Integral Part of Culture

I was confused as to where do I put "Language" while writing about cultural processes. Language, not as English or Hindi, but as the way people communicate with each other to convey organisation specific ideas, opinions etc, is a very important part of culture. And, you should try to learn it as soon as possible on entering the organisation. I would take a few examples

- Acronyms denoting various committees, forums, initiatives
- Technical words, specifications, standards etc.
- Words representing measures and metrics of performance of the organisation or departments
- Designations, roles etc
- Adjectives for characteristics of the product

Understanding Collective Norms, rituals, mores, values and beliefs

We would first begin with explaining each of these different terms.

Norms are explicitly mentioned (not necessarily documented) minimum standards and rules of behaviours – What to wear to offi ce? What are the offi ce timings? How to write emails and other communication? etc. If you follow *Norms* you are considered *Normal* otherwise *Abnormal*. Since norms are explicitly stated you wouldn't have trouble learning them. If you don't follow a norm you would be chastised immediately by your peers, though without serious implications. Find out in your organisation

- What do people wear to office? Formals or casuals?
- What time are you expected to reach offi ce and what time should you leave?

- How do you address seniors – Face-to-face and in emails?
- What are break timings?
- Do people do casual talks in aisles?
- How do people celebrate personal events like birthdays and anniversaries?
- Is it ok to be friendly at work place or strictly professional relationships are maintained?
- Any other norm?

Mores (Mo –Rays) are those norms which cannot be violated without serious repercussions - for example norms around ethical conduct. Mores are usually explicitly written down as corporate guidelines of conduct.

Rituals – in organisations – are ways of doing something in a prescribed way; usually about inducting new comers, departing with exiting members, celebrating anniversaries of important achievements, inaugurating important meetings or events, organising transition events etc. You will understand rituals over time by observing and taking part in them yourself. Since rituals are usually handled by those who are older in the system, you probably would have enough time to learn them before you are supposed to follow them. But, that doesn't diminish the need to learn them consciously.

Values are convictions of people about what is important to them and what is not. It helps them make those decisions which require making trade-offs between two or more different ways of doing a particular thing. For example: An organisation that values Social Responsibility, will not take up a venture that might result in harm to the society in some way. Most organisations have a list of espoused values that they proclaim to follow. However, values in practice might be very different. Values are evident in how senior people prioritise their time, how they make decisions, and how they reward people. Consistently demonstrated behaviours over time can be a firm basis for you to understand the value system of a company. In chapter-2 I had discussed how you may try to make a guess about an organisation's values. You may refer that part again.

Beliefs are assumptions of people about how things are or how things work. A peep into the belief system of people can let you see why people behave in a particular manner. The beliefs could be about self, power, work, time, space, truth and reality, society, environment, and virtually anything.

Belief about self (self as part of the group) could be about capability and weaknesses; they may also be about pecking order and status. These beliefs guide which products and services organisation ventures into, which segment of customers it targets, and whether it takes risk or plays safe. The best place to know this is the Strategic Planning Department.

Belief about power is about the question of centralisation or decentralisation of power. It decides the extent to which employees are allowed to take decisions. Moreover, greater the centralisation of power higher the power-distance: deference showed by the lower rung employees to the senior members.

Belief about work depends to a large extent on the type of work an organisation is involved in. Work could be seen as a mere mean of living or a mean of self-actualisation of potential and creativity. This difference can be easily discerned in the motivation mechanisms employed by the organisation. Often organisations in manufacturing and service industry (even many IT companies) treat work as only a little more than a mean of living. Such organisations have monetary motivators like pay-per-piece and other performance linked incentives in place confirming their inherent belief that money is an effective motivator for work. On the other hand organisations which utilise non-monetary recognition, job enrichment, job enhancement, aspiration management, education support, etc., support the belief that employees want to enjoy the work that they do not for the money that they receive at the end but for the enjoyment and fulfillment that they get while they are at it.

Exhibit 10.2

So Much for Scientific Management

The Father of scientific management, Friedrich Taylor, certainly contributed immensely to increasing productivity and efficiency of the manufacturing industry. Mankind would be forever indebted to him for initiating the scientific study of work place. However, though I am sure he didn't intend to do it, he gave the industry a total non-human outlook. He gave them the belief that work is mechanistic in nature. In increasing the efficiency of production people forgo some basic human needs of the worker. I would take at least two examples

– The Mechanistic view of work laid emphasis on workers achieving expertise in their activities by doing the same thing again and again. It improved efficiency because once the worker has gained expertise he took less time to do the same work. This approach was turned on its head by the Job-Characteristic theory (Oldham-Hackman) which stated that skill-variety is one of the five key characteristics of job that leads to job satisfaction. Moreover it is no news that monotonous job leads to boredom and ennui in long term. Thus the very aim with which the axiom of expertise was adopted is defied due to very human aspects.

– Scientific Management also promulgated the idea of productivity linked incentives. No doubt to some extent it can help improve performance, nevertheless it too has limits. By moving the motivator out of the job externally to money, this approach can take the inherent satisfaction of doing a good job away. The work which could be an end in itself becomes a mean to an end.

Different societies and organisations have different beliefs about time. For some societies it is monochromatic, in which each moment is sequentially connected to the previous one and thus only one thing can be done at a time. This view leads to judicious use of time; interruptions are viewed as loss of time. However, it might also lead to undue stress. For some other cultures time is polychromatic, in which moments have no sequential relationship and many things can be simultaneously done. Interruptions are not considered seriously and are welcomed. In India, time is usually looked upon as polychromatic; queues are often broken here, people in the aeroplanes get up immediately to rush to alight all together, the clerk in the government offices and the local shopkeeper attend to multiple customers at a given time, and so on.

Belief about space in organisations determines how it is distributed based on seniority or some other criterion. Beliefs about personal space, how close you may go to a person without making him feel uncomfortable, also come in this category. In most cultures, personal space is directly linked with power – more powerful you are more personal space you get.

For learning about beliefs of an organisation you need to be patient. By asking, listening and observing you would soon get into the groove. However, if you feel that a particular culture is very different from your own values and beliefs it is time to look out for a change.

Conclusion

Understanding your organisation is key to your performance and success in career. As you enter the organisation ask, listen and observe before judging anything too soon. Look at the organisation structure and organisational socio processes. Try to adapt where it doesn't matter much and try to manage where you could. Nevertheless be sure that you don't work with an organisation with a belief systems contrary to yours. It would be in benefit of both you and the organisation that you leave.

Build Your Network

All successful people have one thing in common: they are well networked. Most of the works in the corporate world get done through networks. Networks provide you information, leads to other important people, advice when needed, and support if required. Networking is an art. It is not the quantity of your connections that matter it is the quality. In this section we will discuss why networking is important and how to develop a strong network that works.

CHAPTER 11

Building a Network That Works

You can make more friends in two months by becoming interested in other people than you can in two years by trying to get other people interested in you.

— Dale Carnegie

There is no job that is truly independent; it is truer for office workers. In fact in complex organisations of today dependency is the way of life. Even at senior levels independence can only be an illusion at best. There is hardly a work in which you could be successful without help from others. Even the individualistic sounding professions – scientists, authors, painters etc. – require an effective network for success[1]. For those of us who work for a company in a regular job – networking can't be ignored. Our works inherently depend on others – for getting information, access to resources, or cooperation in implementation of initiatives. Without others willingly supporting your endeavor, it is sure to fail. Also, these others are not the people within the organisation alone. They also include people outside your organisation – customers, vendors, consultants etc. This group of people makes a lot of impact on the success of your job. In fact your talent can be inhibited or magnified based on your network[2]. Also, more people you know outside your organisation, greater are the chances of getting a job outside – were you to look out for one.

Networking is not about the number of connections you have through exchange of business cards or on virtual networking websites. Nor is it about making deep personal relationships with everyone. What we are about to focus on in this chapter is building a professional network that could help you perform successfully at your job. Some people are naturally adept at building networks and others fumble at the very idea of approaching other people – considering it a difficult task that requires extraordinary inborn skills. Extraordinary skills it requires, nevertheless, can be developed through concerted practice.

Why Network?

Science defines *energy* as capability to do work and *power* as the rate of energy spent. Whenever you get work done some power is consumed. In social set-ups doing work needs power (French, J.R.P., & Raven, B. 1959) – this power could be *legitimate power*, which one derives from one's position; *resource power*, which one derives from control over resources; *expert power*, which is due to expertise in a certain area, *information power*, which is due to access to important information; *reward power* due to authority to distribute rewards; and, *referent power* due to personal charisma. Getting work done through others needs you to possess one power or the other; in different cases you might need different types of power. As a fresher you certainly don't have most of these powers to your credit, and yet you are supposed to get work done through others (even most of the experienced people also don't have all the required power bases). The way out is networking; it provides you with the necessary power to get work done through:

- Providing you access to Information
- Helping you get resources
- Enhancing your creativity through diverse ideas
- Letting you Influence others without authority

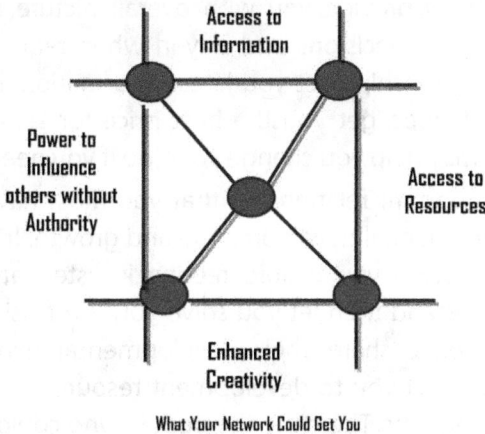

Access to
Information

Power to
Influence
others without
Authority

Access to
Resources

Enhanced
Creativity

What Your Network Could Get You

Figure 11.1

Principles of Networking

Diversify

For being effective your network should consist of diverse people – different from you and different from each other. Many people keep a network that is too similar to themselves. Such a network would not be able to provide you any of the advantages discussed above. People who are too similar to you would have information that you have, would know only those people who you know, and will have ideas too similar to you to help innovation and creativity. Make sure that your network has people from different sociological backgrounds, different expertise, and different organisations.

Diversity also needs to be there in the way you relate with these people: the relationship of give and take. You can divide relationships broadly in three categories and then make sure that you have networks in all the categories.

The first and most obvious relationship is *Professional Relationship*. It consists of colleagues in other departments, seniors at strategic positions, and external professionals. Colleagues help you get your routine work done, seniors at strategic positions provide you with overall picture and also help you get quick decisions and buy-in when required. Your professional relationships get you latest information, help you in solving challenges, get you the best price for services and products, and may help you change your job if you need one.

Another important relationship that you must have is one related to your personal developmental and growth. It includes people who provide you candid feedback, listen attentively to your concerns and then let you solve your professional and personal problems, share their developmental experiences with you, and direct you to development resources like books and training programs. These are the people who could be your mentors or coaches.

One very important relationship is with people who could be your *probable partners* in case you venture out to start something of your own. This relationship usually consist of people who have either supplementary (enhance your effectiveness) or complementary (fill in your gaps) characteristics to your own.

Be Fair

> The Great Sage Confucius was walking through an arid region once with his disciples. Everybody was very thirsty including Confucius. One of the disciples found some water in a rain puddle; he took it in a bowl and offered it to him. Confucius said, "This is too much for a single person and too little for everybody." And thus, denied having it at the cost of fairness.
>
> **– Anonymous**

Numerous psychological studies[3] on people have pointed out the very obvious fact that our grand-parents told us from their own wisdom: Human beings value fairness above most values. Relationships that are not based on fair and equitable give-

and-take usually end up soon with a bitter taste in mouth. It is actually difficult to find a sucker who would keep on helping you while you keep on using him. Moreover, fairness has to be genuine, because humans have an uncanny ability to identify fakes.

The idea of fairness is closely associated with 'Reciprocity'. You may look at relationship like a bank account, you can withdraw only as much as you have deposited. Don't try to be the first one to get benefitted from a relationship. Identify opportunities where you may offer help to others and then do it generously.

Customise

The final piece of advice that I have to offer here is to customise your attitude towards different relationships, once you have diversified it enough. Different people have different needs in at least three aspects of relationship:

Frequency of touch

How frequently do you get in touch with those who you know? Some people can be contacted quite frequently after you have reached certain degree of closeness with them. Other people might be too busy to get time out for such frequent interactions. You need to balance it – the frequency should neither be too overwhelming nor too distancing.

Level of intimacy

How close physically or emotionally do you get to people? It also depends on the culture of a society. In some societies it is ok to be too near and in some others some degree of distance is always maintained. Always maintain a distance that is not too uncomfortable to the other person.

Type of exchange

People are different from each other in their notion of fair dealing. For some people "Thank you" is a very important exchange when they have helped you; for some other people it would be very clear on what tangible thing they need in return of the favour they do to you. It is very essential to understand what others require in order to make a fair exchange. Reciprocity should not only be done; but it should also seem to have been done.

Some Caveats and Conclusion

Organisations are political entities and this fact of life should not be underestimated. As a newcomer to the organisation – as for a stalwart also – there are some caveats to be remembered while connecting with people. Making compromise with these caveats is rife with dangers.

Be discreet when you sound your opinion: "*Walls too have ears*"is an old Hindi saying. In organisation setting, it is difficult for a conversation to remain private for long. Don't be too eager to utter that "truth" to a trusted colleague. It is in your own interest to keep your opinions and judgments about others with yourself – even if someone is probing.

Don't over-rely on a few connections: Though trust is a great virtue; you should be smart enough not to over-rely on one connection for a critical work. Make a network rich enough to have more than one connection in a department or other organisation for important agenda items. I learnt this lesson when I was in touch with just one person in a consulting organisation. When he left, it took a long time for me to get another connection who I could rely on with the same level of trust.

Good might not beget good always: Don't help others with expectations of getting favour in return. But this should not dissuade you from helping others. Sometimes people will back-stab while you did everything to help them. Let them act according to their nature and you stick to your own.

Keep in touch: You will meet people and part ways. Make it a habit to keep in touch with people. Remember personal occasions – birthdays, anniversaries, etc, – and wish people. Use technology to keep in touch. Show interest in people and you might get life-time friendship in return.

No one is useless: Remember the famous poem by the poet Rahim *"Na Jane Kis Bhesh Mein Narayan Mil Jaye"*. Don't ever judge any person as useless. Everybody is important in one way or the other. *"Be humble"*.

Manage Your Career

Successful career more often are not accidents. They are crafted through sincere, concerted, and conscious effort. They form when you understand the god-sent gifts you have, your values, and, most important, your calling. There would be many people on whom you will depend, many you will partner with, and many you would have to fight with to realise your potential. Till then you have to persist..persist..and..persist.

CHAPTER 12

Be Your Own Guide

I still meet young Engineer and Management Trainees with the same old question – "What's going to be my career path?" The question has been asked so many times that it has started looking like a perfectly genuine and legitimate question. Nevertheless, I still believe that this question is absolutely abdicative. I know that if I ask this question to somebody else then it means that I am handing over my life in somebody else's hands. In reality, my career is no one's but my responsibility. Asking this question to someone else is preposterous and shameful.

Organisations can provide opportunities – not career paths (though many organisations claim otherwise). Building of a career stems from your own active efforts. It is you who has to decide what you wish accomplished, what you aspire to achieve, and where you want to head. If the organisation takes these decisions on your behalf, then it would only be serendipitous if you build a career that is in line with your aspirations. In a study[1] published by McKinsey in 2007, most of the people who had experienced a significant defining career change in their lives ascribed it to three top reasons – Realisation that they had become interested in another function or industry; a new job opportunity at the same or other organisation; and, a realisation that their current job had become less attractive. None of these three reasons suggests that the career was designed by the organisation in which these executives worked. It was their inner calling coupled with decision to seize the available opportunity that effected the shaping of their careers. Also, remember that opportunities favor the prepared mind. In this last concluding chapter we will discuss how you could guide yourself in building a career that would let you live a more fulfilled life.

Look into the mirror

We started this book with chapter on knowing yourself as the first step towards preparing yourself for a job that would keep you happy and successful. And if you took the advice and really went ahead taking a few psychometric tests, taking feedback from others, and doing some self-reflection to understand your strengths and weaknesses, it is really commendable. But, don't feel that you can stop there. It was just the beginning. Personalities change over time, self-concept is subject to change with different experiences that life puts you through. Victor Frankl famously said in his classic book A Man's Search for Meaning that you are not there to question life but rather to answer the questions that it puts before you. All of us keep answering these difficult and often complex questions and while we do it we find out new things about ourselves – new talents, hidden blind-spots, unique idiosyncrasies, inborn penchants, deeply detested *bête-noire* and so on. And, as we explore ourselves we develop a self-concept which also defines our career identity[2]. *Looking into the mirror* requires you to have your own unbiased, clear, and an honest mirror that would tell you what you are. The mirror could be – your achievements, your failures, your suppressed desires, your friends, and your family. As you proceed in your career, stop from time to time to reflect in these mirrors. This reflection will let you see if you are in a job that helps you become more of you, more authentic. But don't keep lingering in reflection. It is action that lets you explore more of you. So keep experimenting and reflecting alternately – more action-less reflection.

Keep Developing Yourself

In his other book *Man's Search for Ultimate Meaning*, Victor Frankl said that all freedom had a *"from what"* and a *"to what"*. The *"from what"* is being driven and *"to what"* is being responsible. I thus feel that freedom means: *Being responsibly ambitious*. Ambition doesn't convert into reality until you take responsibility for it. In your career, in order to sustain, you need to develop yourself almost continuously. Growth is not optional it is an imperative. There is a famous principle called Peter's Principle: *People in organisations get promoted up to their level of incompetence.* In order to delay this ceiling defined by your incompetence level, you need to keep preparing yourself for the level above you. The knowledge and skills that brought you so far will not take you to the next level. Promotion is not an entitlement. You get promotion when you have demonstrated that you got what it takes to move up.

There is one more thing that I would like to share -*You either move up or move down*. Status Quo doesn't exist in nature. Don't think that you can remain where you are. It would just not happen. Stagnancy inevitably leads to decay.

Always remember whether you are a tiger or a deer, you better keep running if you wish to sustain. Don't let the feeling of having arrived ever come. If you start feeling arrived, it is sure that you are ready to depart.

Remember the *"Future Resume"* that we discussed in the chapter-3; you need to make a similar resume after joining the job as well. Look further down 5 years and write down:

- What would you be doing after five years?
- What would have been some of your achievements by then?
- What Projects would you have worked on?
- What skills would you have mastered?
- What knowledge base would you have built up?

- What certifications would you have got?
- Which training programs would you have attended?

The future resume will provide you a master plan to move further and work toward making it a reality. Arrive at an action plan for making it true. A sample plan is provided here for your guidance.

Table 12.1

S. N	Resume item	What needs Be Done? (examples provided below)	By When
1	Projects	– Installation of a key part of a power plant.	05.12.2015
2	Skills	– Project Management	05.01.2016
3	Knowledge	– Latest technology in Power Plants	05.12.2016
4	Certifications	– Project Management Professional	05.01.2017

Go it slow

If you were to reach peak of Mount Everest or any other high peak using a helicopter, you wouldn't be able to survive there for long. It is because your body would not have got adapted to the thin air at high altitude. On the other hand if you ascend slowly your body gets adapted to the low pressure levels and you can stay there for elongated times. A similar phenomenon is applicable to growth in your career also. Fast upward leaps are often not secure, it is slow and gradual movement that includes a mix of vertical and lateral movement that ensures success[3]. Go it slow and pick the skills required at each level during your journey. So that when you reach the summit you will be able to sustain the success and live up to the responsibilities that you are entrusted with.

Challenge yourself

> But there is suffering in life, and there are defeats. No one can avoid them. But it's better to lose some of the battles in the struggles for your dreams than to be defeated without ever knowing what you're fighting for.
>
> -- **Paulo Coelho**

Growth happens when you put before yourself challenges that you have never attempted before. It is only through this path that you can explore and actualise your potential.However, facing challenges is not an easy task; it is very easy to give up on the way. Following suggestions might help you

- Although challenges should not be easily achievable they should be within reach if you stretch yourself enough. Unrealistic and unachievable goals can do more harm. They can result in self-doubt and loss of self-esteem and confidence. Thus take moderate challenges that push you to stretch you.

- Don't be under the impression than challenges are always used to improve upon weaknesses. Great masters take challenges in the area of their strength. You also follow it. Taking challenges in the area of your strength are less likely to result in failures.

- Stretch should be alternated with relaxation. That is what the weight-lifters do to develop their muscles.

- Find a coach; it could be a senior colleague who you respect for a particular skill.

- Read biographies of hardy people. They are a source of great inspiration and motivation.

Conclusion

I am sure you would have got quite a few take-aways from this book but don't take them as prescriptive. There is no mathematical equation that could take into account all the variables of life. Go about your worklife with a childlike approach. It is *ok* to burn your hands before understanding what exactly "Hot Saucer" means and to fall down stairs to understand gravity. It would be no fun if someone someday hands you over a book that prescribes an ideal and fool-proof answer to each of your challenges. Life would be banal and full of boredom if you didn't hold your head a few times in frustration. Work would be devoid of meaning if you knew the standard way of doing it every time. Relationships would be eventless and unmemorable if there were no conflicts and difference of opinions. Human Beings would be mechanical and lack vitality if they could become perfectly rational. Look forward to facing the reality – for it is what makes life worth living.

I would like to conclude this book with a little truth very different from what I have discussed in the entire book. Many times while running after success we miss out on the little joys of life. I feel it is very sad that very often for people career becomes an end in itself. Build a career by all means but not at the cost of your life. According to an article[4] in BBC recently, working for more than 10 hrs a day increases chances of heart attack by neary 2/3rd. Life is a much bigger canvas than career alone. No doubt that career is an important part but it is a part nevertheless. In pursuance of your career goals do not forget to live your life. Don't immerse yourself so much in work that you don't get time for your family, friends and yourself. Take vacation, read a fiction, watch movies, go out for a dinner with loved ones, play games, be a child, and let yourself loose for some time.

Go ahead and be *yourself*!

References

Introduction

1. http://en.wikipedia.org/wiki/List_of_universities_in_ India (retrieved on 17th October 2011)

2. http://www.managingpeoplebook.com/ WarForTalentNeverEnded.pdf (retrieved on 5th October 2011)

3. http://planningcommission.nic.in/plans/planrel/ fiveyr/11th/11_v1/11v1_ch5.pdf (retrieved on 5th October 2011)

4. Goleman, Daniel (1998). *What Makes a Leader*, Harvard Business Review, November-December 1998

5. Konnikava, Maria. http://blogs.scientificamerican.com/ guest-blog/2011/08/23/lessons-from-sherlock-holmes-paying-attention-to-what-isnt-there/ (retrieved on 23rd October 2011))

Chapter 2

1. Holland, John L. *Making vocational choices: A theory of vocational personalities and work environments (3rd ed.).* Odessa, FL, US: Psychological Assessment Resources. (1997). xiv 303 pp.

2. Jung, Carl Gustav (August 1, 1971). *Psychological Types (Collected Works of C.G. Jung, Volume 6)*. Princeton University Press. ISBN 0-691-09770-4.

3. http://www.businessweek.com/managing/content/ feb2008/ca20080219_805385.htm (retrieved on 23rd

October 2011)

4. Gardner, H. (2011 edition). Frames of Mind: The theory of multiple intelligences. New York: Basic Books. Tenth Anniversary Edition with new introduction, New York: Basic Books

5. http://www.marshallgoldsmithlibrary.com/cim/articles_ print.php?aid=877 (retrieved on 17th October 2011)

6. http://en.wikipedia.org/wiki/Modularity_of_mind (retrieved on 21st October 2011)

7. http://pzweb.harvard.edu/pis/hg_mi_after_20_years. pdf (retrived on 17th October 2011)

8. Drucker, Peter F. "Managing Oneself." Harvard Business Review 77, no. 2 (1999): 64-74

9. http://www.d.umn.edu/~kgilbert/educ5165-731/ Readings/experiential-learning-theory.pdf (retrieved on 18th October 2011

10. http://en.wikipedia.org/wiki/Need_theory (retrieved on 23rd October 2011)

11. Nash, Laura L., Stevenson, Howard H. *"Success that Lasts".* Harvard Business Review; 102-109, 2004.

Chapter 3

1. Madrigal, Alexis. *Forget Brain Age: Researchers Develop Software That Makes You Smarter* (2008).Wired (http:// www.wired.com/science/discoveries/news/2008/04/ smart_software)

2. Stanovich, K. (2009). Rational and Irrational Thought: The Thinking that IQ Tests Miss. Scientific American Mind. Nov/ DecChapter 5

Chapter 4

1. http://insight.kellogg.northwestern.edu/index.php/m/ article/performing_best_when_it_matters_most (retrieved on 17th October 2011)

2. http://www.kelloggs.co.uk/pressoffice/Content/114/ Benefits_of_breakfast.pdf (retrieved on 17th October 2011)

3. http://articles.chicagotribune.com/2011-01-13/news/ ct-met-talk-test-stress-0114-20110113_1_test-stress-worries-exam (retrieved on 4th October 2011)

Chapter 5

1. Hanna, Julia (2010). *Power Posing: Fake it until you make it*, HBR Research and Ideas (http://hswk.hbs.edu/item/6461. html)

2. http://insight.kellogg.northwestern.edu/index.php/ Kellogg/article/biases_that_bind (retrieved on 21st October 2011)

3. Williams, L. E., & Bargh, J. A. (2008). Experiencing physical warmth promotes interpersonal warmth. Science, 322(5901), 606-607. doi:10.1126/science.1162548

4. Harvard University. "Tactile sensations influence social judgments and decisions." ScienceDaily, 25 Jun. 2010. Web. 18 Oct. 2011.

Chapter 7

1. Bennis W. and Thomas R. (2002) Crucibles of leadership. Harvard Business Review, Sept: 39-45

2. Thomas, Robert J. (2008)*Crucibles of Leadership: How to Learn from Experience to Become a Great Leader* ,Harvard Business School Press

3. Ashkenas, Ron(2011). http://blogs.hbr.org/ashkenas/2010/02/ using-crisis-response-factors.html (retrieved on 22 May 2011)

4. Amabile, Teresa & Kramer, Steve. (2011) http://blogs.hbr.org/ cs/2011/04/four_reasons_to_keep_a_work_di.html?cm_sp= most_widget-_-blog_posts-_-Four%20Reasons%20to%20 Keep%20a%20Work%20Diary (retrieved on 18th Oct 2011)

Chapter 8

1. Buckingham, Marcus & Coffman, Curt W. (1999). *First*

break all the Rules:What the World's Greatest Managers Do Differently(1ˢᵗ Edition, 1999). Simon & Schuster.

2. http://www.mckinseyquarterly.com/Why_good_bosses_tune_in_to_their_people_2656 (retrieved on 18th October 2011)

3. Cross, Rob & Thomas, Robert(2011). http://hbr.org/2011/07/managing-yourself-a-smarter-way-to-network/ar/2 (retrieved on 23 July 2011)

4. Bernstein, Douglas A. & Nash, Peggy W. (2006).*Essentials of Psychology*(Fourth Edition, 2006)Wadsworth Publishing.

5. http://en.wikipedia.org/wiki/Emotional_labor (retrieved on 18th October 2011)

6. Lieberman, M.D., Eisenberger, N.I. Crockett, M.J., Tom, S.M.,Pfeifer, J.H. and Way, B.M. (2007) "Putting Feelings Into Words:Affect Labeling Disrupts Amygdala Activity in Response toAffective Stimuli." Psychological Science, Volume 18, No 5, 2007

7. Ray, Rebecca D., James, Gross J. & Wilhelm, Frank H.(2008). *All in the Mind's Eye? Anger Rumination and Reappraisal.* Journal of Personality and Social Psychology, 2008, Vol. 94, No. 1, 133–145. (Accessed online at http://spl.stanford.edu/pdfs/Ray_08.pdf on 18th October 2011)

8. http://www.psypress.co.uk/ek5/resources/pdf/chap18.pdf (retrieved on 18th October 2011)

9. Csíkszentmihályi, Mihály (1990). *Flow: The Psychology of Optimal Experience.* New York: Harper and Row.

Chapter 9

1. Amabile, Teresa & Kramer, Steven(2011).*THE PROGRESS PRINCIPLE: Using Small Wins to Ignite Joy, Engagement.* Harvard Business Publishing

2. Covey, Stephen R (1990). *Seven Habits of Highly Effective People*(1990).Free Press; 1st edition (September 15, 1990)

3. Schwartz, Tony & McCarthy, Catherine (2007). *Manage your energy, not your time.* Harvard Business Review. October 2007,63-73 (http://hbr.org/2007/10/manage-

your-energy-not-your-time/ar/1)

4. http://www.bnet.com/blog/time-management/can-you-learn-willpower/641?tag=mantle_skin;content (retrieved on 18th October 2011)

5. Sirota, David, Mischkind,Louis A. and Meltzer, Michael Irwin (2005).*The Enthusiastic Employee - How Companies Profit by Giving Workers What They Want.* Wharton School Publishing.

6. http://www.basex.com/web/tbghome.nsf/23e5e39 594c064ee852564ae004fa010/ea4eae828bd411be8 525742f0006cde3/$FILE/CostOfNotPayingAttention. BasexReport.pdf (retrieved on 18th October 2011)

7. Steel, Piers (2010).*The Procrastination Equation: How to Stop Putting Things Off and Start Getting Stuff Done.* Harper

8. http://en.wikipedia.org/wiki/Implementation_intention (retrieved on 18th October 2011)

9. Halvorson, Heidi Grant (2011). http://blogs.hbr.org/cs/2011/02/nine_things_successful_people.html (retrieved on 18th October 2011)

10. http://news.bbc.co.uk/2/hi/uk_news/4471607.stm (retrieved on 18th October 2011)

Chapter 10

1. Mintzberg, Henry (1980).*Structure in 5's: A Synthesis of the Research on Organization Design*, Management Science, Vol. 26, No. 3. (March 1980), pp. 322-341

2. Handy, Charles(1996).*Gods of Management: The Changing Work of Organizations.* Oxford University Press, USA (1996)

3. Maccoby, Michael (1997).*The Gamesman: The New Corporate Leaders*, Simon & Schuster (1977)

4. Training Manual – Technology of Participation, Facilitative Leadership Program Module 3 – Institute of Cultural Affairs, Australia (2008)

5. Wendlandt, Nancy M and Rochlen, Aaron B (2008). *Addressing the College-to-Work Transition, Implications for University Career Counselors*. Journal of Career Development, Volume 35, No. 2, 151-139 December 2008

6. Schein, Edgar H. (2004).*Organizational Culture and Leadership* (Third Edition), Jossey-Bass (2004)

Chapter 11

1. Berns, GregoryDr.(2008).*Iconoclast – A Neuroscientist Reveals How to Think Differently*. Harvard Business School Press (2008)

2. http://insight.kellogg.northwestern.edu/index.php/ Kellogg/article/collaboration_and_creativity (retrieved on 19th October 2011)

3. http://en.wikipedia.org/wiki/Ultimatum_game (retrieved on 19th October 2011)

Chapter 12

1. What Shapes Career – A Mckinsey Global Survey, McKinsey Quarterly (2007)

2. Ibarra, Herminia (2003).*Working Identity - Nine Unconventional Strategies For Reinventing Your Career*, Harvard Business School Press (2003)

3. Hamori, Monika (2010)*Job-Hopping to the Top and Other Career Fallacies.* Harvard Business Review, July-August 2010

4. http://news.bbc.co.uk/2/hi/health/8674372.stm (retrieved on 20th October 2011)

Annexure 1

Assessment 1
How well do I know the campus selection process?

Put True or False against each statement

1. False
2. True
3. True
4. True
5. False
6. False
7. False
8. False
9. False
10. False
11. False
12. False
13. False
14. True
15. False
16. True
17. True
18. False
19. False
20. True

Assessment 2
How well do I know the world of corporate?

Put True of False against each statement.

1. False
2. False
3. False
4. False
5. False
6. False
7. False
8. False
9. False
10. False
11. False
12. False
13. False
14. False
15. False
16. False
17. False
18. False
19. False
20. False

CHANAKYA
Rules of Governance by the Guru of Governance

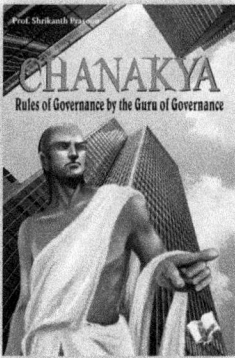

Author: Prof. Shrikant Prasoon
Format: Paperback
Language: English
Pages: 248
Price: ₹ 175.00

Chanakya was both a destructive and creative thinker able to annihilate an established empire and erect and establish another larger, richer and greater on the debris, without money, material and man. So, he is the only qualified person in human history to be Guru; Acharya; Teacher; Guide and Mentor in the field of Management. With his super mind and supreme determination he succeeded in everything and everywhere; and wrote down everything without inhibitions or secrecy for the posterity in his three monumental works:

1. Teachings of Kautilya's Arthashastra & Nitishastra
2. Perfect Analogy between Ancient Managerial System & Modern Corporate Setup

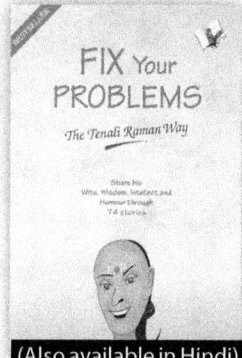

FIX Your PROBLEMS
The Tenali Raman Way
Share his Wits, Wisdom, Intellect and Humour through 74 stories

(Also available in Hindi)

Author: Vishal Goyal
Format: Paperback
Language: English
Pages: 228
Price: ₹ 150.00

Tenali Raman was a court jester, an intelligent advisor and one of the ashtadiggajas (elephants serving as pillars and taking care of all the eight sides) in the Bhuvana Vijayam (Royal Court) of the famed Emperor of Vijayanagar Empire (City of Joy) in Karnataka – Sri Krishna Deva Raya (1509-1529), the model ruler par excellence to Ashoka, Samudra Gupta and Harsha Vardhana. Tenali Raman was an embodiment of acute wit and humour and an admirable poet of knowledge, shrewdness and ingenuity. In a short span, the legacy left behind by Tenali Raman attained eternity. All these qualities of Tenali Raman have been fully explored and displayed in this collection of vibrant fables and anecdotes.

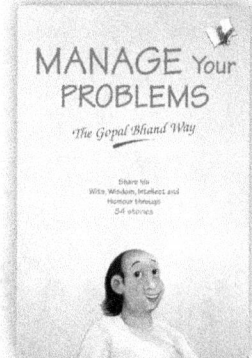

MANAGE Your PROBLEMS
The Gopal Bhand Way
Share his Wits, Wisdom, Intellect and Humour through 54 stories

Author: Vishal Goyal
Format: Paperback
Language: English
Pages: 228
Price: ₹ 175.00

A contemporary compilation of anecdotes Gopal Bhand for 21st Century youth in an engaging blend of wisdom and wit with social and managerial significance. The book comes packed with mind-blowing snippets to keep readers thoroughly submerged in good humour till the end of the book! It is a racy assemblage of earthly wisdom and sparking humour punctuated with moral and mind blowing perceptions to keep today's readers glued to the book looking for more and yet more!.

Marketing for Beginners

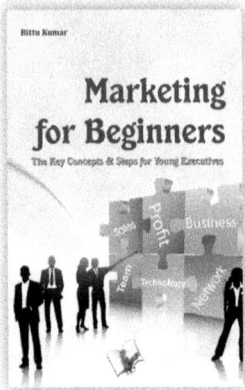

Author: Bittu Kumar
Format: Paperback
Language: English
Pages: 136
Price: ₹ 120.00

"The aim of marketing is to know and understand the customer so well, the product or service fits him and sells itself."

— *Peter F. Drucker*

The book, Marketing for Beginners gives an exhaustive explanation about the key concepts of marketing, its strategies, and defines the important terminologies, such as Brand Selection, Distribution Channels, Vendor Selection, Pricing, Sales Process, Customer Relationship Management(CRM).

It's different and exclusive from other Marketing or Management books as it not only gives the detailed description of the various components of Marketing, but also cites examples to explain each of them, making it crystal clear to the readers.

Winners' Podium

Author: Anchit Barnwal
Format: Paperback
Language: English
Pages: 168
Price: ₹ 200.00

Just as a winning podium can accommodate anyone on it, each one of us is capable to be a winner, irrespective of our shortcomings and differences. Winners' Podium – Everyone Fits on it, attempts to do just that: make out a winner amongst each one of us.

This book offers elaborate guidelines for a balanced, successful and happy living. It tells how one can find his talent, attract ideas and be successful, both personally and professionally. It also talks of happiness and the steps to it.

Through stories, anecdotes, quotations, examples and day to day observations, this book can inspire you to not only attain that most desirable success, but also to hold on and grow both internally and externally with it.

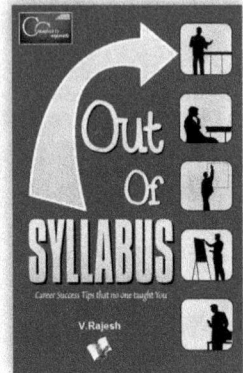

Out of Syllabus

Author: V. Rajesh
Format: Paperback
Language: English
Pages: 104
Price: ₹ 120.00

It is easy to skip a question during an exam if it is "Out of Syllabus" but what do you do if you are faced with a situation in life for which you were not given any inputs? Can you run away from the situation using the "Out of Syllabus" excuse?

Career is one area where one is expected to know and manage situations. After all a person is paid a salary to be able to handle things and deliver results. The reality is that most people get a lot of academic and conceptual inputs relating to one's career choice but very little practical inputs on how to effectively use the academic learning.

visit our online bookstore: **www.vspublishers.com**

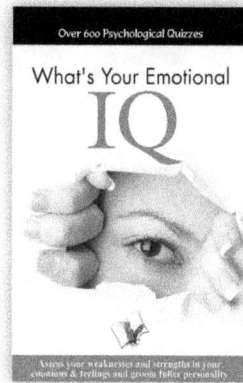

www.ingramcontent.com/pod-product-compliance
Lightning Source LLC
Chambersburg PA
CBHW070419270326
41926CB00014B/2852